CW00555159

Alastair Sawday's
Special Places to Stay

PARIS
HOTELS

2nd EDITION

*"Yet with these April sunsets, that somehow recall my buried life
and Paris in the spring, I feel immeasurably at peace, and find
the world to be wonderful and youthful, after all."*

T.S. Eliot

ASP

Alastair Sawday Publishing

ACKNOWLEDGEMENTS

For the first edition I allocated nearly all the credit to Ann Cooke-Yarborough. For this edition I should allocate it ALL to her. I have only uttered an occasional word of encouragement and helped with the tiny amount of editing and proofing that she generates.

The beauty of this book is that it is the personal selection of one very interesting woman, one who 'feels Paris in her skin' (as she would put it). After living for 30 years both on the edge of the city and in the Loire, she is now rooted in the heart of Paris. And, having tramped the streets in pursuit of these hotels, she has 'the knowledge' - as a London taxi driver might put it. Her views on what makes a hotel special are what makes the book itself special. If you have used her 'French Bed and Breakfast', also published by us, you have also – I imagine – learned to trust her judgement.

Paris hoteliers are generally a tough lot, but the ones who have made it to these pages are among the few who have retained the human touch - and who have communicated that to their hotels and staff. Ann has the human skills, and sheer determination, to establish the relationships that have made this book possible. Add a sophisticated irony, a firm grasp of history and culture, and a deep sense of sheer fun... and you have someone whose views on how to enjoy your precious time in Paris are worth listening to.

Alastair Sawday

Series Editor:	Alastair Sawday
Managing Editor:	Ann Cooke-Yarborough
Researcher:	Ann Cooke-Yarborough
Assistant Researchers:	Brendan Flanagan, Lucie Nérot
Production:	Julia Richardson
Data processing/admin:	Ann Cooke-Yarborough
Cover design:	Caroline King
Colour illustrations & symbols:	Celia Witchard
Cartoons:	John Pruen
Furniture drawings:	Mathias Fournier
Back-up photographs:	Eliophot, Aix-en-Provence (16, 52); Thierry Beghin (2); Ann Cooke-Yarborough, Julia Richardson
Accounts:	Sheila Clifton, Movita Clutterbuck, Maureen Humphries

DISCLAIMER

We make no claims to pure objectivity in judging our special places to stay. They are here because we like them. Our opinions and tastes are ours alone and this book is a statement of them; we cross our fingers and hope that you will share them.

We have done our utmost to get our facts right but apologise unreservedly for any mistakes that may have crept in. Sometimes, too, prices shift, usually upward, and 'things' change. We would be grateful to be told of any errors or changes, however small.

INTRODUCTION

Emerge from the metro virtually anywhere in central Paris and you will find something beautiful before your eyes and interesting people to observe - researching this book has been almost pure pleasure. The metro is comfortingly warm in winter and metro travellers can be a fascinating study in contemporary social styles; there is also a splendid 'choice' of music down there, from the professional rock 'n roll band to the lonely blues guitarist to the struggling Conservatoire student quartet. Working in Paris in August is a treat: the city is empty of Parisians and, more to the point, of their cars, and one can travel by bus along the harmonious avenues.

Tramping the streets to discover new hotels and owners has brought other rewards - unknown little streets, hidden gardens, stunning buildings and courtyards, unusual people and unspoilt cafés. Paris is a buoyant, stimulating environment and I am grateful for every opportunity to dig deeper into its riches.

PARIS HOTELS

Our first edition of *Special Paris Hotels* spoke of an endangered species: the Paris hotelier who blends individuality, warmth and professionalism. Three years later, he/she still exists but is rarer. Small hotels that have been run by the same family for several generations are finding the struggle against chains, great and small, tougher every year. The younger generation often does not want to take over the family business - too much hard work for too little return. So what do the owners do with their hotel when they retire? They look up all the tempting offers they have received from hotel chains and choose the lucky purchaser. And there goes another *Special Place to Stay*.

But all is not lost, as I hope this new edition will prove. Some children DO want to continue the family tradition and are bringing their youthful enthusiasm, married to a 1990s business approach, to the job. Some younger, newer owners are taking a liking to the profession and creating their own mini groups with a handful of charming small hotels. They are also setting up marketing associations with like-minded owners and are genuinely committed to keeping the kind of hotels we look for, with character and the personal touch, open and flourishing.

Lastly, there are a few 'chains', owned by a number of business partners rather than by any one family, who say their intention is to buy up, refurbish and run small hotels with real personality in direct competition with the soulless anonymity of the 'corporations'. The proof of their declarations is in their managers, who stay in place for years and treat hotel, staff and clients as if they owned the place!

What else has changed since 1995?

The most perceptible trend is the inexorable climb towards more technology. People are being drawn into it by the demand, which they ignore at their cost (so they believe), for air conditioning, more luxurious bathrooms, satellite television and computer connections in every room. They are finding it hard to stay simple. If you, too, deplore the priority given to hardware and canned communication over personal attention and a genuine smile, do express your appreciation when you receive these precious gifts. The givers need all the encouragement they can get.

The Second Edition

We hope you will find that the new paragraphs on Making the Most of Paris are a useful addition to the basic hotel information and that our illustrated guide to French period furniture styles will bring added light to your reading of the entries and spice to your stay in your chosen hotel.

Inclusion

What I have said above gives the main clue to how we choose hotels: we have to LIKE them. Some have declined to pay the small fee we charge to feature in this book, often (a real sign of these new, internetted, times) because they are now relying solely on their website to tell the world about their hotel. Some declined because they are planning a total overhaul in the next two years. But most of the previous entries whom we invited back have been happy to join in the second edition and some who refused the first time are here now.

PLEASE let owners and managers know that you are an Alastair Sawday reader. They may even have something special for you.

John Pruen's cartoons

They are here for you to enjoy - and perhaps learn a bit of French from. John Pruen drew them to make his own learning more fun. They have only ever appeared in print in this book.

GENERAL FACTS OF PARIS HOTEL LIFE

Space

The luxury of luxuries in Paris is **SPACE.** Hotel rooms tend to be small so we tell you where there are exceptions to this rule. If you try a selection of our 3-stars you will experience the enormous variety in space per person per room.

Service

The second luxury is **SERVICE**. Parisians are intense, intelligent, ambitious - and attentive to themselves(!). So, when you meet a really friendly hotelier or receptionist, do tell them how much you appreciate their attitude. It is exceptional. We have tried to keep it as a basic criterion for selection but the same people do not work at the desk all the time and the same person may not always be as sunny. We have eliminated some potentially good hotels because the telephone reception was surly, the management systematically absent leaving an unhappy minion to hold the fort, or our encounter too cold to invite further contact.

We, and presumably you, infinitely prefer a welcome that is polite but warm and relaxed, to the coldly obsequious yet snooty treatment that 'palace hotels' appear to consider is appropriate to their status.

BUT, 'ours' are all small hotels, chosen for their friendliness and simplicity. They have small staffs and cannot really be expected to provide gin and tonic or lobster at 2am.

Telephones

With few exceptions, all rooms have telephones, more and more with direct dialling; some can even supply a private line with your own number. There are also increasing numbers of modem sockets in Paris hotel rooms, for those who cannot bear to be cut off from Global Communication of Everything. Remember, however, to use hotel telephones only in extremis or if you are rich. The bills rarely fail to raise eyebrows, and temperatures.

Our telephone numbers give the ten-digit number every French subscriber now has, e.g. *(0)1 23 45 67 89*.

- when dialling from *inside* France from any public or private telephone, dial all ten digits, including the bracketted zero, i.e. *01 23 45 67 89*;
- when dialling from *outside* France, use your international access code then the country code for France - *33* - followed by the *last 9 digits* of the number you want, e.g. *00 33 1 23 45 67 89*;
- numbers beginning *(0)6* are mobile phone numbers and will cost you accordingly;
- to telephone <u>*from France*</u> - <u>*to Great Britain*</u>, dial *00 44* and your correspondent's number *without its initial zero*, <u>*to the USA*</u>, dial *00 1* and your correspondent's number *without its initial zero*.

Family suites

Most hotels can turn two double rooms into a self-contained suite so do enquire when booking.

Bathrooms

Almost all bathrooms have wc's so we have only indicated the exceptions. Also, most baths have shower fittings, though not always with curtain or screen. Where some have just shower, we have said so. Be prepared for the smallest cubicle in some of the cheaper hotels (and even in some of the others).

Noise

Noise is a general problem in Paris and we cannot claim that every one of these hotels is silent. Late-night revellers under your window (or, more annoyingly, a stream of cars) is often part of the package. More and more hotels are fitting double glazing and air conditioning but if you are a fresh air fiend and can't sleep with the windows shut, bring your earplugs. Or ask for a room *sur la cour* (over the courtyard) - it probably won't have a stunning view but it will be quieter. The other noise problem, in the cheaper hotels, can be internal, caused by thin walls and televisions - or those late-night revellers on their way to bed.

It's hard to know what to do about this but earplugs are still one answer. You could also try asking to change rooms the next morning for a quieter end of the corridor.

Breakfast
There is continental, continental plus and buffet. 'Continental' is the very basic coffee/tea/chocolate with *baguette*, butter and jam and possibly a croissant. 'Continental plus' is all this plus yoghurt or cheese, fruit or fruit juice, other pastries or more varied breads. Buffet means anything from continental + eggs to a vast spread worth breakfast, lunch and half of dinner at once. Buffet breakfast is served... at the buffet. If you choose to have breakfast in your room it will probably be continental. Because of the lack of space, Paris hotel breakfast rooms are often in their stone vaulted cellars. Magnificent examples of a well-tried building principle, they are, of course, 'authentic', 'original', 'fascinating', but they can be rather stuffy and close.

Pillows and tea
If there is something you need and can't see, ASK for it. The hotel may or may not be able to provide but you can only find out by asking. If you don't like the bolster they have put on the bed, look in the cupboard for a pillow. If it's not there, ask. If only coffee is offered for breakfast and you need tea, ask for it; don't suffer in silence for the duration of your stay. A teabag should always be forthcoming. (Tip: take your own favourite tea-bags with you!)

Parking
We tell you which hotels have their own car parking arrangements, but do not take these for granted: space must be booked at the same time as the room. The charge will be between 80Frs and 150Frs per day.

Tipping
Don't be bullied! Only tip if someone has made a special effort for you.

TECHNICALITIES

English
English, *of some sort or another*, is spoken at all these hotels - it is a condition of their survival, though in the smaller, simpler places, you may be greeted by an assistant or a member of the family who is not the mainstay of the establishment. Be prepared to forgive some rather halting English in such cases and make generous use of sign language.

The star rating system
It is misleading. The majority of small Paris hotels have three official stars. They are allocated once only (unless the hotel asks for reassessment) by a totally bureaucratic measurement of square centimetres of bathroom, walking space round beds, number of taps per person, and so on. So the 3-star group contains the sublime and the disastrous; 4 stars should be better than 3 but some of our 3s are more luxurious - in space, quality of welcome, attention to detail - than certain 4s; and we have 2-stars that merit more but don't want to be jumped up into the all-embracing 'superior' category. Judge for yourselves.

Prices

In general, we print advertised standard rates. Most hotels offer reductions for low-season bookings (August, July, mid-winter), some all year round, a few principled places never. Always ask but better not to press. And let owners and managers know that you are an Alastair Sawday reader. Some may have a special deal for you.

The prices printed here are for 1999. Anyone travelling beyond 1999 should expect changes.

Millenium's Eve

You must not be shocked at considerable price hikes during the last week of 1999 - hotels in desirable places the world over will be doing this, I fear.

Taxe de séjour

Paris City Council levies a tax per person per night in Paris hotels. It is currently 3Frs for 1-star, 5Frs for 2-star, 6Frs for 3-star, 7Frs for 4-star. Some hotels include it in the price, some add it on - we can't specify which so be prepared for a small extra sum per day on the bill.

Credit cards

There are only three hotels in this book which don't take credit cards: Esmeralda, Nesle and Port Royal (reminder in each text). Most of the others take all cards but do check for exceptions when booking.

Booking Services (Services de Conciergerie)

All 4-starred, most 3-starred and some lesser-starred hotels will make bookings for theatres, restaurants, trains, etc, but only the 4-starred are bound to do so.

Currency Exchange

The smarter hotels have an exchange rate board at reception; others will give you francs for your own currency as a personal service; some won't touch it. In all cases, you will get a worse rate than at the bank and you can always get francs out of a cash distributor with your Visa card.

Room Coding System

S - single; D - double; TW = twin; TR = triple; Q = quadruple; DP = duplex; APT = apartment; ST = suite i.e. EITHER a Full Suite = two rooms (sitting and sleeping), plus bathroom OR what is called a Junior Suite = one very large room with a comfortable sitting area, plus bathroom.

YOUR COMMENTS

We include a report form at the back of the book. We are eager for all kinds of feedback. Please write, however briefly, and tell us your experiences, good or bad, in 'our' hotels and your reactions to this guide. We really WILL pay attention.

CONTENTS

Montparnasse - Luxembourg

Hôtel Beauvoir	5	24
Hôtel Istria	14	25
Hôtel L'Aiglon	14	26
Hôtel Raspail Montparnasse	14	27
Hôtel Novanox	6	28
Le Sainte-Beuve	6	29
Hôtel Le Saint-Grégoire	6	30
Hôtel Ferrandi	6	31
Hôtel Normandie Mayet	6	32

St Germain des Prés - Orsay

Le Madison	6	33
Hôtel Luxembourg	6	34
Hôtel Louis II	6	35
Hôtel de l'Odéon	6	36
Hôtel du Globe	6	37
Le Relais Saint Germain	6	38
Hôtel Saint André des Arts	6	39
Hôtel de Nesle	6	40
Welcome Hôtel	6	41
Hôtel de Seine	6	42
Hôtel des Deux Continents	6	43
Hôtel des Marronniers	6	44
L'Hôtel	6	45
Hôtel de l'Académie	6	46
Hôtel de l'Université	7	47
Hôtel de Lille	7	48
Hôtel Bersoly's Saint Germain	7	49
Hôtel Verneuil	7	50
Hôtel Bourgogne et Montana	7	51

Invalides - Eiffel Tower

Hôtel de la Tulipe	7	52
Hôtel du Palais Bourbon	7	53
Eiffel Park Hôtel	7	54
Hôtel du Champ de Mars	7	55
Hôtel Relais Bosquet-Tour Eiffel	7	56
Hôtel Le Tourville	7	57

Trocadéro - Passy

Hôtel Frémiet	16	58
Hôtel Passy-Eiffel	16	59
Hôtel Massenet	16	60
Hôtel Gavarni	16	61
Les Jardins du Trocadéro	16	62

Plan of Paris Metro System

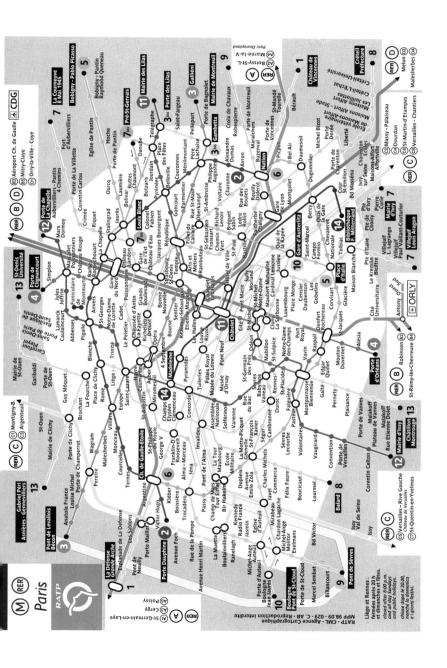

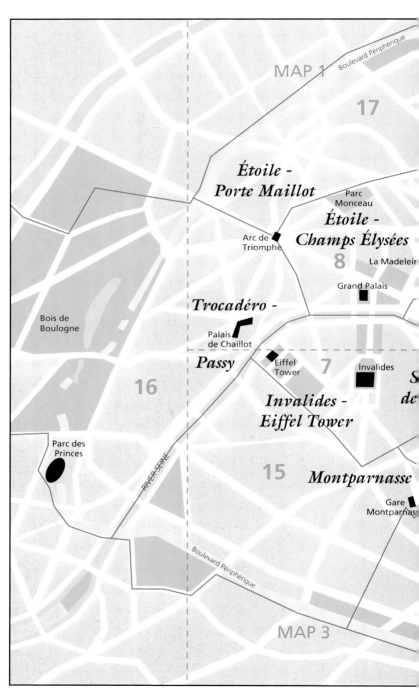

Paris - General Map with Arrondissements

Detailed maps are shown on the following pages.

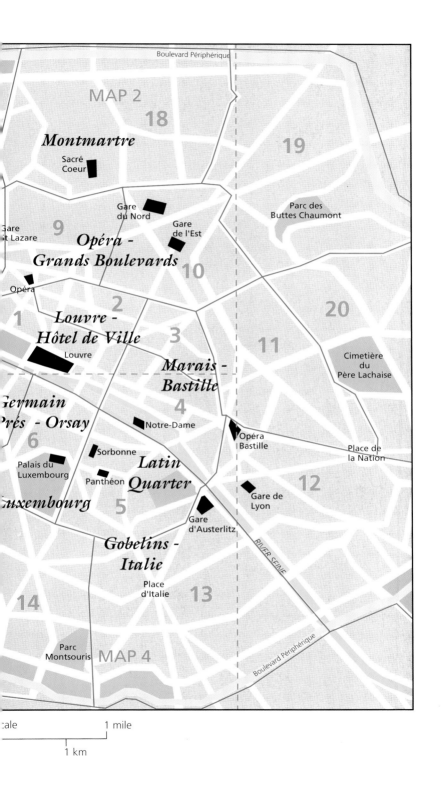

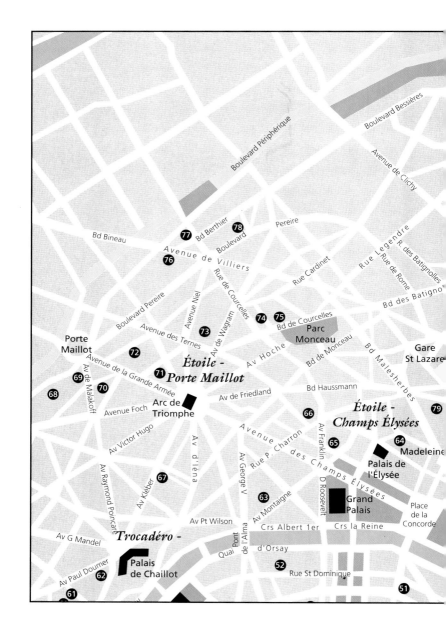

MAP 1

Scale

1 mile

1 km

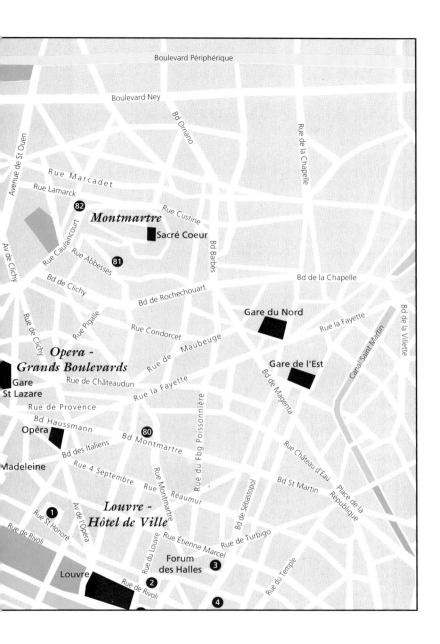

MAP 2

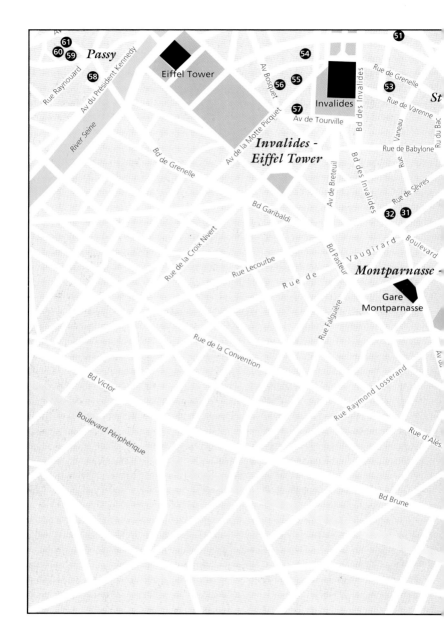

MAP 3

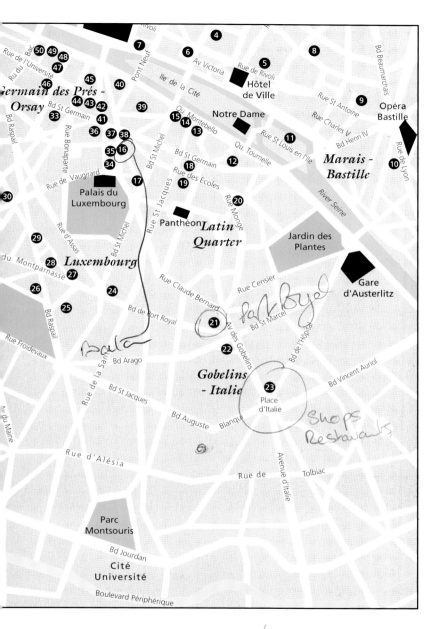

MAP 4

SYMBOLS

Treat each one as a guide rather than a concrete indicator. A few notes:

A green leafy spot. It might be a tiny bright-white plant-filled lightwell; very occasionally it is a fully-fledged garden

English spoken by receptionist and management, but not necessarily by the other staff.

Pets are accepted as long as they are properly trained and docile. There may be a supplement to pay.

Lift installed. It may stop short of the top floor or start on the first floor.

Bar. There is a bar or simply bar service.

Mini bar in bedrooms.

Restaurant. The hotel has its own restaurant or a separately managed restaurant on the spot or next door.

Room service for light meals (or more) delivered to your room by outside caterers or the hotel kitchen.

Double glazing. Rooms (on street side at least) have double glazing or double windows.

Air conditioning in bedrooms. It may be a centrally-operated system or individual apparatus.

Television set in bedrooms.

Satellite television in bedrooms.

Hair dryer in bedrooms.

Safe in bedrooms or individual safes at reception (otherwise you can leave your valuables at reception).

Disabled facilities provided.

Louvre – Hôtel de Ville

Hôtel des Tuileries
* * *

10 rue Saint-Hyacinthe
Paris
75001

Tel: (0)1 42 61 04 17
Fax: (0)1 49 27 91 56

Management: Jean-Jacques Vidal

At the charming Tuileries you will find a family atmosphere, a very personal approach to interior decor and a friendly welcome. The many oriental rugs — most of them on walls — sit well in such a lovely quiet old building (it is a *Relais Silence* hotel) whose façade moves skywards to the rhythm of balconies, arches and mouldings while huge old doors give onto a white hall with rugs, mirrors, pictures old and new, leading to a pair of small, elegant, sitting areas. A pretty, planted lightwell illuminates this ground floor space and the basement breakfast room. The curving generous staircase has an old-fashioned central runner and brass rods on polished wood and though the orientalising element is fairly general it is never excessive; there is a room like a soft Persian tent while another has a clever, original draping of yellow cloth over white bed. There are Chinese-vase table lamps, Chinese-inspired wallpaper, paisley curtains. Care has been taken over colours — a white room has dark blue carpet, pale blue damask curtains and bedcover with a richly coloured rug on the wall behind the delightful cane bedhead. The bedside lighting is good, there are some pretty antiques and country pieces plus modern elements. One room has an interesting long narrow dressing table in carved painted wood and Empire bed and armchairs (remember Empress Josephine...). Finally, mattresses are excellent and the marble bathrooms most acceptable. 4 family apartments can be created and the higher prices are for the excellent de luxe rooms.

Rooms: 26 with bathrooms.
Price: S 790-990F; D/TW 890-1400F.
Breakfast: Buffet 60F.
Meals: No.
Metro: Tuileries, Pyramides; RER Opéra-Auber.
Bus routes: 72
Car park: Place Vendôme, Marché St Honoré.

The house was built for one of Marie-Antoinette's ladies-in-waiting; the supremely elegant, feminine façade and great carved front doors, both listed, are admirable indeed.

Tonic Hôtel Louvre   ★★

12-14 rue du Roule
Paris
75001

Tel: (0)1 42 33 00 71
Fax: (0)1 40 26 06 86
E-mail: tonic.louvre@wanadoo.fr

Management: Frédéric Boissier

Don't come to the Tonic for exciting interior design, but people appreciate its superb Right-Bank position between Seine, Louvre and the Châtelet-Halles shopping centre; its steam-and-whirlpool baths, too, are a boon after a conscientious tramp round the Louvre or, if you really have to, round Disneyland. Despite the new rich blue colour of the desk, the lobby still feels a bit bare but the friendly, energetic receptionists are ready to help with any practical questions and the very comfortable armchaired, ground-floor breakfast room/bar looks onto life in the quiet street. Frédéric Boissier, sticking to his principles, provides wholemeal breads and low-fat dairy products and refuses basement breakfast because it does nothing to stimulate you for the day. The hotel is in two adjacent buildings that communicate along the pavement. The older, more "traditional" half has more style and slightly higher prices. The hall here is old and gracious, the staircase, crafted in an unusual long curved V, is listed. Your legs will recognize the centuries-worn oak nosings and terracotta tiles (there is a lift too). Rooms, sparse and functional, have decent storage space, high beamed ceilings, some old stone walls, copies of Louis XIII furniture and no pictures. Rooms on the "modern" side have the same fully-equipped *tonique* bathrooms plus the basics of table, chairs and room to move around. On the top floor there's a sense of light, a sloping ceiling and a balcony onto St Eustache, floodlit at night.

Rooms: 34 with whirlpool and steam bath (except 2).
Price: S 590-890F; D 690-1200F; TR 840-13500F.
Breakfast: 50F.
Meals: No.
Metro: Pont-Neuf, Louvre-Rivoli. RER Châtelet-Les Halles.
Bus routes: 21 67 69 72 74 75 76 81 96
Car park: St Eustache; Les Halles.

In Rue de l'Arbre Sec, the ancient Dry Tree Inn, named after an evergreen in Palestine that lost its leaves the day Christ was crucified, used to receive Holy Land pilgrims.

Map No: 2

(2)

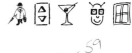

Hôtel Agora ✦✦
7 rue de la Cossonnerie **Tel:** (0)1 42 33 46 02
Paris **Fax:** (0)1 42 33 80 99
75001

Management: Monsieur Fresnel, Monsieur de Marco

Look well, oh traveller — you'll find the door between hot dog shop and bank, under the feathery acacias of the pedestrian area. You are greeted by a delicious cherub at the bottom of an elegant grey staircase. Old and modern are married throughout: alongside a sober contemporary desk there is an elaborate gilt mirror, a carved armchair, a cloth monkey in a gilded cage, a plaster virgin in a glass box and plants galore. The welcome combines old-fashioned grace and modern friendliness in this gentle *salon* overlooking the lively street — I loved the feel. The tiny breakfast room is to scale, its huge floral pattern less so. All the rooms are different, some smaller than others, none very big; all give onto the street, all have double glazing but if you sleep open-windowed, ask for a high floor. Beds have firm foam mattresses, curtains are all white, towels good for the price. There are choice C19 engravings everywhere, such as a very full-fleshed Judgement of Paris offset by a demure Virgin Mary. Nothing is standard or mass-produced. Colour contrasts abound too: yellow red-flowered wallpaper with blue frieze plus blue carpet and bedcover in No 51 which has a lobby with cupboards, a balcony and a superb view of St Eustache. There are fine, carved, gilded, wall-mounted bedheads; one room has puce paintwork, soft mauvy walls and a leopard-skin chair. It all works admirably — really! The touch is very sure. Bathrooms are colourful and adequate. Really excellent value so close to the Pompidou Centre.

Rooms: 29 with shower or bath.
Price: S 345-485F; D 530-590F.
Breakfast: 40F.
Meals: No.
Metro: Les Halles; RER Châtelet-Les Halles.
Bus routes: 38 47
Car park: Les Halles.

The cage once held live birds, banned since American animal rightists stayed here during their campaign against the French fur trade and used gentle persuasion...

Map No: 2

3

Hôtel Saint-Merry   * * *

78 rue de la Verrerie
Paris
75004

Tel: (0)1 42 78 14 15
Fax: (0)1 40 29 06 82

Management: Monsieur Crabbe

Lovers of the Gothic, seekers of the utterly unusual, this is for you! Once the presbytery, this hotel snuggles so closely up to the lovely Late Gothic church of St Merry that the back bedroom walls are the church's stone façade. In the suite, the great clock tower cornice thrusts its way into the sitting room, and elsewhere a pair of flying buttresses provides the most original of bed canopies. M Crabbe has laboured for 35 years, trawling every *brocante* and flea market, to make the old house worthy of its origins. By reworking old pieces (mostly C19 neo-Gothic), he and his cabinet-maker have created a custom-made Gothic environment of which he is rightly proud. In the 1st-floor reception, the All-Gothic takes over: high-backed chairs, an elaborate pew, linen-fold cupboard doors, telephone behind part of a confessional. Monsieur greets you with attention and enthusiasm. To set off the festival of dark carving, his rooms are all soberly decorated with original beams, terracotta tiles, plain velvet or 'medieval-stripe' curtains and bedcovers, wonderful cast-iron light fittings, and some surprisingly colourful bathrooms. Some have views up to the Sorbonne. The cheaper ones are small and basic. The suite with its private staircase, big be-timbered sitting room (the only Gothic *salon* in Paris?), cosy bedroom and fascinating bathroom (mind your head getting out of the bath), is a masterpiece of style and adaptation. NB. Difficult motor access in this pedestrian street and no lift in hotel.

Rooms: 9 + 1 suite with bath or shower
& wc; 2 with shower, sharing wc.
Price: D sharing wc 450F; D or TW
800-1100F; ST 1800-2400F.
Breakfast: 50F (served in bedroom).
Meals: Wide choice of eating houses at
your doorstep.
Metro: Hôtel de Ville, Châtelet; RER
Châtelet-Les Halles.
Bus routes: 38 47 75
Car park: St Martin.

One of Paris's finest C15 Gothic churches, Saint Merry is also home to a very C20 pastoral encounter and action centre for the less privileged members of the consumer society.

Map No: 2 & 4   (4)

Hôtel de Nice ★★

42bis rue de Rivoli
Paris
75004

Tel: (0)1 42 78 55 29
Fax: (0)1 42 78 36 07

Management: Monsieur, Madame & Marie Voudoux

You cannot but warm to the Voudoux and their lovely little hotel, at one of the hubs of the city. Both left high-flying professions to indulge their dream of running a 'guesthouse' together and their daughter is happy to be joining the team. It will feel like home for many: Indian cotton covers on beds, kilims on floors, a vast portrait of Lady Diana Cooper on one wall (bought, unknown and unmounted, for her beauty and style), innumerable prints, engravings and mirrors on others and a remarkable sense of hospitality — the fundamentally French art of intelligent conversation is still alive. The discreet door is blue, the hallway and stairs decorated with deep red bookbinding paper, turquoise paintwork and C19 perspectives of capital cities, some wildly imaginary (e.g. Peking-on-Sea). Rooms have pretty Laura Ashley papers copied from French C18 designs and mix 'n match curtains, old doors on built-in cupboards (Monsieur has a passion for old doors, polished or painted), portraits of ancestors and old bedside lights. None of the rooms is very large but storage space is adequate for sensible travellers; bathrooms, also quite small, are modern and properly equipped. If the hosts and the public areas are fairly exotic, the bedrooms are fresh, individual and restful. All overlook a typical Parisian square with cafés, benches and plane trees just off the Rue de Rivoli. This may be a little noisy if you need to open your window, but double-glazing does work and the Nice is excellent value.

Rooms: 23 with bath or shower.
Price: S 380F; D/TW 500F.
Breakfast: 35F.
Meals: No.
Metro: Hôtel de Ville; RER Châtelet-Les Halles.
Bus routes: 47 69 72 74 76 96
Car park: Baudoyer or Lobeau.

In nearby Rue du Bourg Tibourg is the beautiful 1830s shop where Mariage Frères sell innumerable teas in black tins and serve wickedly tempting cakes in the tea room.

Map No: 4

Hôtel Britannique   ✱ ✱ ✱

20 avenue Victoria
Paris
75001

Tel: (0)1 42 33 74 59
Fax: (0)1 42 33 82 65
E-mail: mailbox@Hotel-Britannique.fr
Net: www.Hotel-Britannique.fr

Management: J-F Danjou

In the very middle of Paris, on the one quiet street beside the Châtelet, several generations of British (*Britannique*) Baxters owned this well-placed comfortable hotel and ran it exclusively for British clients. The present owner is an ex-naval man with a passion for Turner — the great painter's 'Jessica' greets you from her window in the lobby, copies of his oil paintings and water colours adorn the bedroom walls and the 'Fighting Temeraire' dominates the saloon-like sitting-room, alongside a model galleon, a 'Crystal Palace' birdcage housing a lone dove and an EMI gramophone horn. There is a lush feel about the hallways but do use the staircase rather than the lift; it is elegantly pink and grey with handsome original fitted oak chests on each landing. The rooms, some a decent size, some quite small, are decorated with well-designed built-in elements, pastel walls, grey-green leaves and red grapes on curtains and quilts, boxes of pot-pourri for extra florality and perfectly adequate bathrooms. I liked the modern double-framed mirrors too. The higher floors have views over the surrounding roofs and treetops. On the avenue below, garden plants, furniture and birds are still sold — it's fun in the daytime. The semi-basement breakfast room, lit by a glass roof, has a wall cabinet where you can admire a silver teapot presented to the Baxters "at Whitsuntide 1861 by their Scarborough friends". It is simply comfortable with no ancient flourishes and a generally very friendly reception.

Rooms: 40 with bath or shower.
Price: S 725F; D/TW 872-998F; extra bed 126F.
Breakfast: 61F for a copious buffet.
Meals: No.
Metro: Châtelet; RER Châtelet-Les Halles.
Bus routes: 21 38 47 58 75 76 81
Car park: Hôtel de Ville.

During the 1st World War, the hotel was offered to American and English Quaker volunteers tending civilian victims — a service rendered by the Quakers in wars the world over.

Map No: 4   (6)

(some)

Le Relais du Louvre ***

19 rue des Prêtres St Germain l'Auxerrois
Paris
75001

Tel: (0)1 40 41 96 42
Fax: (0)1 40 41 96 44
E-mail: au-relais-du-louvre@dial.oleane.com

Management: Sophie Aulnette

An utterly delightful place, with a charming young manageress and views down the throats of Gothic gargoyles! Loaded with history — the French Revolutionaries printed their newspaper in the cellar, and it was Puccini's Café Momus in *Bohême* — the building daily rings with the famous carillon from the belfry beside St Germain church, and beams abound. The lobby is large and colourful in red and green with a low desk for a natural, civilised reception. Antiques and oriental rugs complement the modern advantages of good bedding and fully-equipped bathrooms (a few singles have showers). Streetside rooms look out over *Flamboyant* windows, pinnacles and flying buttresses ("flying buttocks" as I heard a child innocently call them); look left and you see the austerely neo-Classical Louvre. Other rooms give onto a plant and light-filled patio and two ground-floor rooms have direct access. Televisions hide quite rightly in padded stools. The top-floor junior suites have twin beds and a sofa (not convertible, so no cluttering up), pastel walls, exuberant-print upholstery, good storage and heaps of light from their mansard windows. You feel softly secluded and coddled. The magnificent new apartment is big and beautiful with fireplace, books, music, old engravings and a superb verandah kitchen. Other rooms are smaller but luminous, fresh and restful. On each floor, two rooms can become a family suite. The sense of service is highly developed and, as there is no breakfast room, breakfast comes to you!

Rooms: 21, incl. 2 junior suites + 1 apartment, with bath or shower.
Price: S 620-780F; D/TW 850-980F; ST 1300-1500F; APT 2200F.
Breakfast: 50F (in bedroom).
Meals: Light meals 30-100F.
Metro: Louvre-Rivoli, Pont Neuf; RER Chatelet-Les Halles.
Bus routes: 68 69 72
Car park: Card at hotel.

The best view over Paris is just beside you — and it's free! Take the lift to the terrace roof of the Samaritaine store and admire the city from its very centre.

Map No: 4

7

Marais – Bastille

Hôtel de la Bretonnerie ***

22 rue Sainte Croix de la Bretonnerie
Paris
75004

Tel: (0)1 48 87 77 63
Fax: (0)1 42 77 26 78
Net: www.HoteldelaBretonnerie.com

Management: Valérie Sagot

Closed in August. One of the oldest parts of Paris, the original marshland (*marais*) was settled when the islands in the Seine became overcrowded; it escaped unscathed from Baron Haussmann's sweeping C19 town plan and the Bretonnerie has uncovered its C17 timber frame to create a warm, welcoming lobby with daring (and most successful) duck-egg walls. There is space and shape and the wrought-iron, wooden-railed staircase is an elegant reminder of that Parisian talent for grandeur on a human scale. The breakfast room, in a lovely bare-stone vaulted cellar, has subdued lighting and high-backed chairs that add to the Jacobean hideaway feel (there is a second vault below this one!). Upstairs, rooms are reached along twisty split-level corridors, past lacy corners and are all different, some displaying giant structural timbers. Recently renovated rooms have thick cloth walls and curtains and a superior country atmosphere. One large two-windowed twin room on a corner has yellow Jouy-style 'brocade' walls, a rich brown carpet, elegant square yellow quilts across pure white bedcovers (an idea used with style throughout) and a big marble bathroom with matching wall cloth. A smaller double has a delicious orange and yellow colour scheme and a painted cast-iron bed. One fine suite drips pink chintz, old furniture and... space. Bathrooms are good, some are big, and renovation continues. Last but not least, the staff are quite delightful.

Rooms: 30, incl. 3 duplexes and 4 suites, all with bath.
Price: D/TW 650-795F; ST 995F.
Breakfast: Continental plus 55F.
Meals: No.
Metro: Hôtel de Ville; RER Châtelet-Les Halles.
Bus routes: 47 72 74 75
Car park: Baudoyer.

This street, known 700 years ago, was named after a convent built on the *Breton* field where the monks spent their lives meditating on the Passion and Cross of Christ.

Small
48 - 56
inc B/fast

Hôtel de la Place des Vosges ✶✶

12 rue de Birague
Paris
75004

Tel: (0)1 42 72 60 46
Fax: (0)1 42 72 02 64
E-mail: globemar@easynet.fr
Net: www.france-hotel-guide.com/h75004placedesvosges.htm

Management: Philippe Cros

One of the smallest hotels in Paris, its rooms are small too but each has all the essentials. Built at the same time as the beautiful Place des Vosges in whose amicably awesome shadow it stands, this simple and unpretentious hotel has kept its original layout. What you see and live in here is the scale of a successful mule-hirer's house in 17th-century Paris. The old-furnished, comfy reception/sitting/breakfast area, welcomingly hushed after the traffic on nearby Rue St Antoine, was where the mule master tied his mules in days of gentler, cleaner transport (the rings are still there in the old stone walls). The great beams overhead supported the hay loft, above that his living quarters and right at the top his stable boys' garrets. There is an air of relaxed hard work that has come down with the centuries. This implies time to chat with visitors and guide them on their day's programme. Above the ground floor, you must expect less space. The tiny staircase (the lift goes from 1st to 4th floors) precludes large bags as does the pretty minimal storage space in the rooms. Decor is as simple as the atmosphere, pink and beige, old-fashioned satiny bedcovers, with tiny but perfectly adequate shower and bathrooms that are gradually being redone in smart dark green. Up its own little stair, the top floor is an ideal family hideaway with a view of the Bastille column from its attic windows. If you travel light, this is a wonderful part of Paris to be in, rich in history and alive with 1990s Parisians.

Rooms: 16 with bath or shower.
Price: S 385F; D 485-560F; TW 580F; TR/Q 610F.
Breakfast: Included.
Meals: No.
Metro: Bastille; RER Châtelet-Les Halles, Gare de Lyon.
Bus routes: 20 29 69 76 86 87 96
Car park: 16 rue St Antoine.

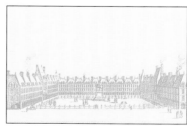

Theme for meditation: the vast beam in the lobby was growing in the soil of France when Charlemagne was crowned Holy Roman Emperor in 800AD.

Map No: 4

Le Pavillon Bastille ***

65 rue de Lyon	**Tel:** (0)1 43 43 65 65
Paris	**Fax:** (0)1 43 43 96 52
75012	**E-mail:** hotel-pavillon@akaMail.com
	Net: www.france-paris-com

Management: Fabienne Fournier

The Bastille area IS trendy Paris; the arty crowd are in the nearby Marais, so the Pavillon's mix of fine C19 townhouse façade and high-modern interior is most fitting. Created from nought, the hotel never deviates from its themes of blue, yellow, music-score lines (*opéra oblige*) and circle segment — it is a sophisticated designer triumph. And moreover... attention to guests is paramount. Thus, you arrive through the front court with its lovely C17 fountain and ring the bell: staff come to you and carry your luggage. On three evenings a week there is wine-tasting in the modern/baroque lobby among the columns, deep blue drapes, tall metal lamps, hanging C16 'masks' and blue-and-yellow leather chairs. Rooms are all alike: small with custom-designed elements and mirrors to make the best of all spaces. The television+minibar unit has a curved mirror on top with a vase of fresh (blue and yellow) flowers under an ultra-mod suspended fragment of light. Bedside lighting is perfect, general and dim, individual and adjustable. Bathrooms have blue and white tile patterns, marble tops, fluffy towels, real glasses. You can breakfast in the vaulted cellar or, in good weather, in the pretty but noisy courtyard. Then cross the road to visit the fascinating array of workshop studios underneath the arches or walk at 3rd-floor height on top, along the leafy Green Stream (*Coulée Verte*) of the disused railway line, the *Viaduc des Arts*. (The higher room price is for extra services — do enquire.)

Rooms: 25 incl. 1 suite, all with bathrooms.
Price: S/D/TW 815-955F; suite 1375F; connecting family rooms available at special rates.
Breakfast: Buffet 70F.
Meals: Light meals 50-100F.
Metro: Bastille; RER Gare de Lyon.
Bus routes: 28 29 63 65 86 87 91
Car park: Opéra Bastille.

The golden genie on top of the bronze Bastille column is presumed to represent Liberty breaking her bonds and sowing the Light into a glorious future.

Map No: 4

Hôtel du Jeu de Paume ★★★★
54 rue Saint-Louis-en-l'Ile
Paris
75004

Tel: (0)1 43 26 14 18
Fax: (0)1 40 46 02 76
Net: www.jeudepaumehotel.com

Management: Elyane Prache

Three storeys soar to the roof timbers of the C17 indoor 'tennis' court: the Jeu de Paume is unique. Smallish rooms, a Provençal style, oodles of atmosphere and genuine attention from the mother-and-daughter team who keep it alive and sparkling. Rooms are all different, with careful pastel/print decor, decent bathrooms and new well-sprung mattresses; beams, real old floor tiles and visible stonework. Duplexes have tiny staircases but more storage than others. Top-floor corner rooms show the building's beautiful beamy skeleton. The fine new duplex-with-terrace is a delight. You love it all or you don't. Love it for its sense of history, eccentricities, aesthetic ironies, secluded peace and feel of home, or you're unhappy with its unconventional attitudes, relaxed staff (plus sheepdog Enzo) and often limited storage space. We love it hugely. Seclusion? You can easily miss the brass plates into the porch. Peace? The hotel is built round a patio garden and all rooms give onto courtyards. Eccentric? Catch your breath at the view from the 2nd-floor glass doors down onto the Provençal tables, the four ex-cloister columns, the fountain and stone cherub — are they indoors or out? The sitting area is a family drawing room: deep leather sofas round a carved fireplace, *objets* and artefacts. And the magnificent high vaulted cellars offer fitness bikes, sauna and a brand new billiards table. A reader wrote: "But what really makes this hotel different is the exceptionally polite, friendly staff".

Rooms: 30 (inc. duplexes) with bathrooms; 1 duplex suite for 1-4 with bathroom, shower room & terrace.
Price: S/D small 905F, standard 1195F, large 1265-1425F; DP 1525F; ST 2400F.
Breakfast: 80F.
Meals: From local caterers 70-250F.
Metro: Pont Marie, Cité, St Paul; RER St Michel-Notre Dame.
Bus routes: 67
Car park: Quai de l'Hôtel de Ville.

The *jeu de paume*, an Italian game that became tennis, was all the rage in 1634. Louis XIII gave permission to develop the island on condition that a palm game court was built. *Plus ça change...*

Map No: 4

(11)

Vivement les vacances.
Roll on the holidays.

Don't forget to bring the washing in!

Sorbonne
•
Pantheon
•
St Séverin
•
St Julien le Pauvre
•
Cluny Museum
•
Rue Mouffetard
•
Institut du Monde Arabe

Latin Quarter

Hôtel de Notre Dame ★ ★ ★

19 rue Maître Albert
Paris
75005

Tel: (0)1 43 26 79 00
Fax: (0)1 46 33 50 11

Management: Monsieur Fouhety

 (1 floor)

On a quiet street in one of the oldest parts of Paris, a stone's throw from Notre Dame, a most attractive red-framed glass frontage opens onto a large lobby adorned with a magnificent tapestry, bits of antiquity, deep armchairs and huge bunches of flowers. The openness is confirmed — these people genuinely like people and greet you with smiles and humour. Beyond the lobby there is a small inviting bar and breakfast area. If the age of the building (1600s) is evident in its convoluted corridors, contemporary style dictates their smart black dados with tan or sea-green uppers. Bedrooms also mix old and new. There are beams and exposed stones, some of them enormous, and cathedral views from the higher floors, though windows are smaller here than on the first floor. (Top-floor rooms now have air conditioning.) Most rooms have a porch-like entrance created by a large curvy 'shelf' that carries the discreet spotlights. The custom-made desk units reflect this design and cupboards often have a useful space for suitcases at floor level. Upholstery is warm and light with soft-coloured suede or small-flowered cotton walls, gentle check or pastelly floral curtains and bedcovers. I liked the translucent Japanese screen doors to bathrooms — an excellent idea for small layouts; not all baths are full size. Redecoration is in progress and the new style is more colourful with yellow, red and blue themes. The black eunuch portrayed as Marie-Antoinette's feathered fan bearer lived here...

Rooms: 34 with bath (exc. 1 with shower).
Price: D 750F; TW 850F.
Breakfast: 40F.
Meals: No.
Metro: Maubert Mutualité;
RER St Michel-Notre Dame.
Bus routes: 47 63 86 87
Car park: La Grange.

On the square at the end of the road on your way to the Notre Dame, two shops: the only patchwork specialist in Paris and a knowledgeable dealer in Native American art and literature.

Map No: 4

Hôtel Esmeralda

4 rue Saint Julien le Pauvre
Paris
75005

Tel: (0)1 43 54 19 20
Fax: (0)1 40 51 00 68

Management: Michèle Bruel

The Esmeralda doesn't change, thank heavens! You feel the whole of Left Bank, artistic, eccentric Paris has concentrated here. Madame Bruel, with cigarette-holder and ethnic-weave jacket, for years a pillar of the intellectual nomad's cosmos, will tell you her fascinating life story at the drop of a hat, show you her work (she's an artist herself), expect you to love her dog and damn all bureaucrats to eternal flames. She still loves her clients, who bring her presents. Her cat is now 20 and the Esmeralda is very old, and dark, and creaky and smelling of polish and dog. It is also noisy, on the edge of the pedestrian Latin Quarter, but what matter when you have Notre Dame on your left (rooms with The View are more expensive than rooms without) and St Julien le Pauvre, the oldest church in Paris, on your right? Up the very fine 1640 staircase, along twisting sloping corridors papered with what look like book illustrations, to rooms that, however small, are also full of character, with florals and fireplaces, chandeliers and ancient bedheads. There are undoubtedly some nice antique pieces (an inlaid sideboard, ornate mirrors), and that includes all the wallpapers... All rooms are different, the largest looking across the Seine to the cathedral; the smallest are like cupboards, facilities basic but perfectly adequate. Few concessions to modernity but massive quantities of atmosphere and encounters with potentially famous showbiz folk if you're lucky(?). Book early — it is VERY popular. No credit cards.

Rooms: 16 doubles with bath or shower & wc; 3 singles with basin, sharing shower & wc.
Price: S basin 160F; D 320-490F.
Breakfast: 40F.
Meals: No.
Metro: St Michel; RER St Michel-Notre Dame.
Bus routes: 21 24 27 38 96
Car park: Notre Dame.

Your lady hostess (+ ex-husband) relaunched the Bâteaux Mouches after the war with an old boat that she painted entirely by hand — "the only real one on the river".

Map No: 4

Les Rives de Notre Dame

* * * *

15 quai Saint Michel
Paris
75005

Tel: (0)1 43 54 81 16
Fax: (0)1 43 26 27 09

Management: Monsieur Degravi & Mademoiselle Grace

Bijou, with just ten rooms. Immense, with the view past the secondhand book stalls to the Seine and the great cathedral. And perfect soundproofing against the traffic. This is special indeed. The owners have brought the colours and textures of Provence and Tuscany to a C16 townhouse. There are ancient beams and superb 'aged' marble tiling; fine ivy-tendril wrought-iron work and delicately painted cupboards by a brilliant Tuscan artisan; masses of dried flowers and other *naturalia*. Light pours into the sitting area from the glass canopy and a forest of plants rises to meet it. Through an arched 'fortress' door, each bedroom has its own combination of sunny southern materials, all in colour coordinations and contrasts that mix flowers, stars and stripes in almond green and flame, or rich blue and *vieux rose* or, for patriots, good old red white and blue. BIG double/twin beds have soft luxy duvets and head cushions hanging from iron ivy stems; each has a table and chairs for intimate breakfasts, a deep sofa and a pretty bathroom. They are a good size (just three on the 1st floor are given for singles but could take couples) and the magnificent top-floor studio is huge; all but one look over the Seine. The welcome is genuinely friendly and relaxed, Grace and her minions have the time and the inclination to be attentive to one and all. "Make yourself at home" is the message, amazingly extended to "Help yourself to extra towels from the landing cupboard". You will feel well cared for in this exceptional house.

Rooms: 10 with bathrooms.
Price: S/D small 995F; D/TW 1650; ST 2600F.
Breakfast: 85F.
Meals: On request 150-200F.
Metro: St Michel; RER St Michel-Notre Dame.
Bus routes: 21 27 38 85 96
Car park: St Michel.

The nearby *bouquinistes*, who sell secondhand books of great or minimal value, old magazines and new postcards, are a radical Parisian institution who resist all attempts to 'organise' them.

Map No: 4

14

Le Notre-Dame Hôtel ★ ★ ★
1 quai Saint Michel
Paris
75005

Tel: (0)1 43 54 20 43
Fax: (0)1 43 26 61 75

Management: Monsieur Fouhety

Up a mirrored staircase from the noisy embankment you will find the reception and an attractive beamed bar on the first floor offering vast views of Notre Dame, the Seine, the booksellers' stands and crowds of students and tourists — this hotel is at the hub of the Latin Quarter (it is the white building in the photograph). Yet the staff will quickly make you feel you belong here. As in a dream, you can study the cathedral's medieval stone wonders from your bedroom window. The window is fully soundproofed for a peaceful sleep (rooms ending in 5 give onto a quiet if dingy courtyard). The rooms are not large but they are uncluttered and full of light from the river, with cane or modern, white lacquer/silver trim, made-to-measure furniture, deep raspberry or pale mushroom cloth on walls, soft print draperies and nice china lamps. The corner rooms (ending in 2) have brilliant round-the-corner views. The duplex rooms are striking. You reach them from a landing with a delightful timber frame + skylight detail. No 63 has an elegant little red sitting room with strong abstract upholstery on the convertible sofa, a gold plush French armchair, a small antique desk, an equally small window and loads of atmosphere. Up tiny stairs (do mind your head) to a sleeping area with full view of Notre Dame from the velux window. The well-designed bathrooms are fashionably marbled or pin-stripe-tiled. Altogether most pleasing.

Rooms: 26 with shower or bath.
Price: S/D 590-790F; DP 1050F.
Breakfast: 40F.
Meals: No.
Metro: St Michel; RER St Michel-Notre Dame.
Bus routes: 24 47
Car park: Notre Dame.

Run out of bedtime reading? George Whitman's world-famous *Shakespeare & Co*, English-language bookshop and meeting place, is just down the road.

Grand Hôtel des Balcons ★★

3 rue Casimir Delavigne
Paris
75006

Tel: (0)1 46 34 78 50
Fax: (0)1 46 34 06 27
Net: www.balcons.com

[handwritten notes: ✓✓ 47-51 Excellent Bfast.]

Management: Denise & Pierre Corroyer

Yes, it is balconied, and moulded, and corniced! But the real originality is in the Art Nouveau interior. Denise Corroyer took the original 1890s windows (don't miss the irises, lilies, tulips and bindweed on the staircase) and copied their voluptuous curves onto panels, screens and light fittings. These being permanent fixtures, she now teaches *ikebana* and uses her art to decorate the public rooms. There is a touch of humour in the lifesize 'negro boy' smiling on a shelf; a touch of eroticism in the full-bodied Venus who supervises breakfast; a sense of lightness and pleasure that owners and staff communicate as effectively as their surroundings. Service is the key word and Jean-François (Jeff to English-speakers), the owner's son, is efficiently enthusiastic about this philosophy: there is now an ice machine, a superior selection of bathroom consumables, a clothes line over every bath, a big luggage room for that last day and a practical, modern meeting room where clients can work or children play. Rooms are far from enormous but judiciously designed table units use the space cleverly, and streetside rooms have, of course, balconies. At the back, you may complain of being woken by the birds! The whole place is in prime condition (an eagle eye is kept and no damage left unrepaired for long), with firm beds, new blankets throughout, good bathrooms, simple, pleasantly bright colours and materials. Afternoon tea and biscuits are offered in winter — and breakfast is a feast which is FREE on your birthday!

Rooms: 55 with bath or shower.
Price: S 405-475F; D or TW 475-515F; TR 580F; child under 10 in parents' room free.
Breakfast: 55F buffet including sausages, ham, eggs, cheese.
Meals: No.
Metro: Odéon; RER Luxembourg.
Bus routes: 24 63 86 87 96
Car park: Ecole de Médecine.

Casimir Delavigne was dubbed a 'national poet' during the turbulent days after Waterloo: he sang about patriotism and "the need to unite now the Foreigners have left".

Map No: 4

Hôtel Le Clos Médicis

★ ★ ★

56 rue Monsieur le Prince
Paris
75006

Tel: (0)1 43 29 10 80
Fax: (0)1 43 54 26 90
E-mail: clos-medicis@compuserve.com
Net: www.paris-charming-hotels.com

Management: Olivier Méallet

With old stone walls and glazed frontage, the Clos Médicis still looks like the shop it was. Virtually rebuilt in 1994, the entrance hall was given light and space by incorporating an old bookshop. As you come in from the excited Boulevard St Michel, you go past a fine stone pillar and an old mirror towards the light of the quiet sunny patio and the reception. On your right is an attractive countersunk area with old beams, a welcoming (winter) fire and comfy armchairs. Muted jazz can be heard; the fashionable window display (red flower pots, green apples and little water-colours when I visited) changes twice a year. This place is very contemporary Parisian yet has its roots in provincial soil: a *clos* is a vineyard and each of the 38 rooms is named after a famous wine. Bathrooms are impeccably fitted and the tiling brings a whiff of Provence. There are pictures in antique frames and old beams throughout, bold patterns and modern colours, wave-shaped bedheads and tall medieval-inspired lampshades, designed by the architect. Some rooms show a sober, masculine elegance; others have more floral tendencies. Room 46 has a Pluto-grey bathroom; No 65 is a nicely-arranged duplex; No 12 has a private terrace. Care has been taken to leave noise out in the street. The fully soundproofed rooms are elegant, not always very big but extremely comfortable. The Beherec family, who also own the Neuville, know how to choose staff who share their lively sense of hospitality.

Rooms: 22 doubles, 16 twins with bath or shower.
Price: D/TW 790-990F; DP 1200F.
Breakfast: 60F with fresh juice, cheese, hard-boiled eggs, fruit salad, prunes.
Meals: On request 100-180F.
Metro: Odéon; RER Luxembourg.
Bus routes: 21 38 82 84 85 89
Car park: Rue Soufflot.

The Prince here was a powerful Bourbon who nevertheless had to whisk his bride away from Paris straight after their wedding in 1609 to remove her from the King's pressing attention.

Hôtel du Collège de France ★★

7 rue Thénard
Paris
75005

Tel: (0)1 43 26 78 36
Fax: (0)1 46 34 58 29

Management: Madame Georges

Excellent value in a favourite neighbourhood, the Collège de France, on a quiet street away from the bustle of the main student drags, has an atmosphere of solid, well-established family comfort — there are exposed stones, lots of wood, soft armchairs by the fireplace in the red *salon* and good lighting. You will be greeted by the utterly delightful Georges couple and by a less animated and considerably older Joan of Arc. The ground-floor breakfast room is warmly red too, with old Parisian prints on the walls and a Madonna in an alcove. The fifth and sixth-floor rooms have balconies on the street side and the rooms under the roof, with their beams and views, are the most characterful, even if you have to walk up from the fifth floor where the lift stops. Indeed, the staircase is worth visiting for its round timbers and its windows encrusted with autumn leaves, a really original touch. Most bedrooms are not very big but each one has new beds this year, a full-length mirror and a thoroughly practical desk unit. With mostly neutral decor — plain walls, smart white bedcovers and richer-coloured curtains — it is both careful and restful and the bathrooms are fine. Several triple rooms and family apartments are possible and, above all, a genuinely friendly reception is assured. You may receive useful vibrations from The Collège, a pillar of the French intellectual community since 1530 where free lectures are given by the great scientific and literary minds of the day.

Rooms: 29 with bath or shower.
Price: D or TW 590F.
Breakfast: Unlimited continental 35F.
Meals: No.
Metro: St Michel, Maubert-Mutualité; RER St Michel-Notre Dame.
Bus routes: 24 63 86 87
Car park: Maubert-Mutualité.

The chemist baron Thénard discovered ultramarine blue (first called Thénard Blue) and hydrogen peroxide and later taught at the Collège de France from 1802 till 1840.

Map No: 4

18

(2 rooms)

Hôtel Résidence Henri IV   ★ ★ ★

50 rue des Bernardins
Paris
75005

Tel: (0)1 44 41 31 81
Fax: (0)1 46 33 93 22

Management: Madame Gernigon

The Henri IV is different — small and intimate at the end of a cul-de-sac, caught in something of a time warp, it provides basic cooking facilities in all its rooms and apartments... and the maid does the washing up! The entrance is through big dark red double doors into a simple hallway where diminutive Ionic columns grace the 'marble' desk and a baby genie of the lamp lights the staircase. Each apartment feels like a French family's home: the original ceiling mouldings and wall panels are still in place, the great marble fireplace with its ornate mirror still dominates the balconied sitting room (the sofa is a modern convertible), the bathroom overlooking a back garden is big and simple (it may have a marble basin or coloured tiles behind the bath), the bedroom has its own little cast-iron fireplace, and there is a slight air of faded grandeur. Furnishings are in keeping with the architecture: thin-legged plush-seated chairs, floral curtains, blue quilts and padded bedheads, an antique writing desk or an old country *armoire*. Some of the double rooms have built-in desk units and pediment-style bedheads, painted in distressed green or beige. The apartments keep their kitchen corner in a little passage, the double rooms in their entrance lobby. All the basics needed for simple cooking are there, without the mess of wet tea towels and sticky soap bottles. With so few rooms, your welcome is calm and attentive. I felt it would be ideal for couples or families wanting to stay a few days.

Rooms: 8 twins, 5 apartments, with bath and kitchenette.
Price: S/D 700-900F; APT 1000-1200F.
Breakfast: 40F.
Meals: Self-catering.
Metro: Maubert Mutualité;
RER St Michel-Notre Dame.
Bus routes: 24 63 86 87
Car park: Maubert Mutualité.

The Bernardin (Cistercian) monks had a college here in the 13th century to teach their recruits St Bernard's rules of simplicity, humility, hard work and true devotion.

Map No: 4

19

Familia Hôtel ★★
11 rue des Écoles
Paris
75005

Tel: (0)1 43 54 55 27
Fax: (0)1 43 29 61 77

Management: Éric Gaucheron

The Familia is well named! And its two official 'stars' are outshone by the glow of care and attention showered upon the house and its guests. Éric is taking over from his parents, who are still very much present, and even if the hotel looks pretty grand from the outside with its balconies and masses of geraniums, their earnest wish is to welcome guests as they would their own friends: enthusiastically. The entrance hall, with its old stone structure, is delightfully decorated with a mural of Paris by an artist friend. Breakfast is taken in the ground-floor room where the family's collection of leather-bound tomes and the thick oriental rug give a homely feel, belied only by the individual tables. This plain and simple atmosphere informs the bedrooms. They are not large or 'Parisian chic' but each has either a lovely fresco of a Paris monument, a wall of ancient stones, an old carved bedhead or a balcony onto the fascinating street life — or a mixture of all this. Carpets, wallpapers, bedcovers and curtains seem somehow comfortingly provincial and solid, not brilliantly trendy or stunningly matched. Bedrooms and the small but adequate bath and shower rooms are being renovated and the whole place is spotless. The balcony rooms are rather special and double-glazing protects them from undue traffic noise. All front rooms look across the wide street to a rich jumble of old buildings with the Ile Saint Louis just beyond. Ask Éric anything — he will answer willingly, at length and in fast English.

Rooms: 30 with bath or shower.
Price: S 390F; D shower 440F; D bath 500F; TW 510-550F; TR 620-660F; Q 730F.
Breakfast: 35F.
Meals: No.
Metro: Jussieu, Cardinal Lemoine; RER Cluny-La Sorbonne.
Bus routes: 47 63 67 86 87
Car park: Lagrange, Maubert Mutualité.

This is a typical *Style Noble* C19 Haussmann building, i.e. it has balconies on 2nd, 3rd and 5th floors. Non-nobles lack the 3rd-floor adornment. Look around you for examples.

Map No: 4

(20)

Gobelins – Italie

Port-Royal Hôtel

*

8 boulevard de Port-Royal
Paris
75005

Tel: (0)1 43 31 70 06
Fax: (0)1 43 31 33 67

Management: Thierry Giraud

The reception/sitting area has doubled in size and comfort behind the new two-arch frontage but the old black fish (saved by the kiss of life from the trauma of change) still dominates his aquarium and the lovely grandfather clock still keeps time. The Girauds have run their hotel for 67 years, have a remarkable sense of service and deserve appreciation beyond any star system. Their information sheets, in 5-star English, are ideal. The hotel is impeccably clean, friendly, unpretentious. If you are broke and don't mind the loo down the passage, take a room with washbasin (some of the communal showers are superb, more expensive rooms have their own bathrooms) and base yourself here, just minutes from trendy Rue Mouffetard with its lively street market and ancient St Médard church (where you can receive absolution for cannibalism) and a short walk from the Latin Quarter. The tree-lined boulevard is leafily Parisian (streetside rooms are double-glazed), there is a dear little inner patio where, in summer, a plain and nourishing breakfast among the plants will set you on your way while the Girauds help you plan your day. Most rooms are fairly small — the general rule in Parisian hotel rooms — with basic furniture, sober decor and adequate beds. There is nothing extravagant, not many pictures, no television ("clients don't want it") and walls are fairly thin, but it is all beautifully kept and they are SUCH NICE PEOPLE. Much praised by readers; wonderful value. No credit cards.

Rooms: 26 with bath or shower & wc;
20 with basin, sharing shower & wc.
Price: S basin 180-225F; D basin 225F;
D/TW bath or shower & wc 335-350F.
Breakfast: 27F.
Meals: No.
Metro: Gobelins; RER Gare
d'Austerlitz, Port Royal.
Bus routes: 27 47 83 91
Car park: Patriarche.

So close to the Santé prison, the hotel was used overnight by priest and executioner before their 5am (public) appointments with Mme Guillotine and her unhappy prey.

Map No: 4

21

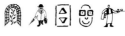

Hôtel Résidence Les Gobelins   **

9 rue des Gobelins
Paris
75013

Tel: (0)1 47 07 26 90
Fax: (0)1 43 31 44 05

Management: Monsieur Poirier

The street, the hotel, the owner are all quiet and unassuming — no need for double glazing — and the patio is a real gift. This was a neighbourhood of modest dwellings for people working at the great Gobelins tapestry workshops and was never very smart. But it is near the entertaining, slightly Bohemian Rue Mouffetard with its little eating houses, big mosque, lively market and left-wing culture. The lobby/lounge, with simple rattan furniture and thick cushions, and the airy breakfast room, decorated with much-loved black and white photographs of Paris and Parisians, lie round a pretty, honeysuckle-hung, plant-filled, courtyard where tables and chairs invite you to relax under the friendly eye of two small Burgundian lions. The rooms are as simple as the rest and there is enough space. Nothing superfluous can be detected yet all the essentials are there, on a basic theme of pastel-coloured walls, white piqué or striped Indian cotton bedcovers, a writing table and chair and a decent cupboard. Some have been redecorated more recently than others, some wallpapers need redoing; Monsieur Poirier plans to transform the look gradually into something less hotelly and more individual. All the rooms are quiet and light though party walls seemed rather thin. The gentle unobtrusive friendliness reminds the sensitive guest that this used to be a *pension de famille*; it has kept that incomparable sense of intimacy and understanding.

Rooms: 32 with bath or shower.
Price: S 325-395F; D/TW 395-465F; TR 565F.
Breakfast: 38F.
Meals: On request 50-150F.
Metro: Gobelins; RER Port Royal.
Bus routes: 27 47 83 91
Car park: Place d'Italie.

Gobelins is the great name of great French tapestries but the Gobelin brothers were, in fact, simple dyers and the streams here ran blood red from their labours. Tapestries came later.

Map No: 4   (22)

Hôtel La Manufacture ★★

8 rue Philippe de Champagne
(Avenue des Gobelins)
Paris
75013

Tel: (0)1 45 35 45 25
Fax: (0)1 45 35 45 40

Management: Géraldine Le Bobinnec

The newest, smartest two-star hotel in Paris! In a genuinely Parisian residential neighbourhood, full of *brasseries* and little shops — do visit the Butte aux Cailles, one of the last of the old 'villages' — and just ten minutes from the Pantheon and Montparnasse. Opened in September 1998, it was first stripped and then virtually rebuilt; the name, of course, refers to the great *Manufacture des Gobelins*, just up the road, where fabulous tapestries have been woven since the 17th century. Deep raspberry is the house colour (all the carpets tell you so) and developments on the theme are inventive without being overstated — it is all deliciously fresh and speaks of summer in the country. On the oak-boarded ground floor, you find an attractive bar, sitting corners with coral-coloured chairs and sofas, and a breakfast area of red-checked benches and rush-seated chairs. The rooms, mostly small but perfectly planned, and with big windows, are colour-themed and upholstered for a fresh, simple look: red, yellow, pink and blue coordinated in little flowers, fine checks or classic Jouy designs. Let us know what you think of the clever custom-made MDF furniture. The top-floor (more expensive) rooms, with their sloping ceilings and bigger bathrooms, are more generous in space, light and views. Ask for a room looking over the *Mairie* or the courtyard rather than the police station. Many of the new bath and shower rooms have windows. Altogether an excellent addition to the Paris hotel scene.

Rooms: 57 with bath or shower.
Price: S 420-550F; D 460-600F;
TW 500-650F; ST 750-800F.
Breakfast: 42F.
Meals: No.
Metro: Place d'Italie; RER: Gare d'Austerlitz.
Bus routes: 27 47 57 67 83
Car park: Free parking nearby.

Philippe de Champagne, the epitome of a court painter, lived in Marie de Médicis' royal palace, had a handsome income from her and was a founding member of the Academy of Painting.

Map No: 4

Luxembourg Palace and Gardens

•

Odéon Theatre

•

Montparnasse cemetery & cafés

•

Place de Catalogne

Montparnasse – Luxembourg

(some)

£83

Hôtel Beauvoir   * *

43 avenue Georges Bernanos   **Tel:** (0)1 43 25 57 10
Paris   **Fax:** (0)1 43 54 31 87
75005

Management: Monsieur Atmoun

Why Beauvoir? Because Simone, the brilliant companion of philospher Jean-Paul Sartre, used to stay here. Hemingway lived here for a year too; their favourite haunt, the Closerie des Lilas (now a lot more expensive than in pre-war days), is just across the way. Less glamourously, the Beauvoir looks down onto the 'Chinese pavilion' that is Port Royal station and the tracks; fear not though, the RER (Suburban Express Railway) is renowned for its amazingly silent trains. Inside, the large ground floor, with its magnificent half-timbered, wooden-stepped staircase, contains reception, sitting and breakfast areas that were attractive enough when I saw them, with a little green well like a stage set at the back, but rather tatty: refurbishment is due this winter and I met the designer who plans to tile the floor, brighten the walls, change sofas, chairs and tablecloths. It has great potential. Rooms are to be redone too, with new carpets, desks, etc. Rooms on the street have a fine view of the 'Petit Luxembourg' garden (the main garden is just beyond). They are all plain-painted or pastel-stripe wallpapered with bright blue paintwork, pale upholstery, pretty curtains and ginger-tiled bathrooms. Although small, they provide for all your needs if those needs are simple and, as at the Normandie, there are very attractive prices for our readers with a 10% reduction in High Season (HS) and real bargains in Low Season (LS in 'Price' below) i.e. January, February, March, July and August.

Rooms: 29 with bath or shower.
Price: S 345F (ASP readers LS 300F);
D 395F (ASP readers LS 340F);
TW 495F (ASP readers LS 380F).
HS less 10% for ASP readers.
Breakfast: 35F.
Meals: No.
Metro: Vavin; RER: Port Royal.
Bus routes: 38 83 91
Car park: Montparnasse.

Port Royal convent made itself famous (notorious?) for reforming its VERY lax ways and becoming the cradle of Jansenism, which preached austerity as the only true habit.

Map No: 4   (24)

Hôtel Istria ★ ★

29 rue Campagne Première
Paris
75014

Tel: (0)1 43 20 91 82
Fax: (0)1 43 22 48 45

Management: Daniel Crétey

Superbly placed for transport from airports, mainline stations and the attractions of lively Montparnasse, yet secluded in a quiet back street, the Istria has a string of famous names on its books — those rather wild arty people who lived, loved and worked here in the heyday of Montparnasse's avant-garde scene. The hall now promises peace and quiet with its deep leather sofas and tartan-upholstered French chairs; fame comes in the shape of a small wooden Charlie Chaplin sitting benignly in the corner. The new owners (Monsieur is delighted to take time to chat to his guests and guide them to the best of Paris, Madame is more behind the scenes) have kept the plain, simple, good-quality furnishings and decor. Thus, the contemporary bedroom furniture made of gently-curved round-edged pieces of solid elm, specially designed for the Istria by Jacques Athenor, will just be brightened with new curtains and more modern table lamps. The same discreet, simple taste prevails in the bedroom decoration where palest yellow Korean grass paper may cover the walls and pale mauve cloth stretch across the bed. The showers (there are 4 baths in all) are delightful quarter-circle constructions; the beds have slatted bases and firm new Dunlopillo mattresses. The lovely stone vaulted breakfast room still has its blue check tablecloths and soft lighting. Charm and thoroughly good value for a 2-star hotel near Montparnasse.

Rooms: 26 with shower or bath.
Price: S 400-500F; D 500-600F.
Breakfast: Continental plus: 40F.
Meals: On request c. 100F.
Metro: Raspail, RER Port-Royal .
Bus routes: 68 91
Car park: Montparnasse.

The Istria was immortalised by Louis Aragon in a poem to his beloved Elsa; Duchamp invented his "readymade" art here; Man Ray took pictures — enough glory?

Map No: 4

Hôtel L'Aiglon ★★★

232 boulevard Raspail
Paris
75014

Tel: (0)1 43 20 82 42
Fax: (0)1 43 20 98 72
E-mail:.hotelaiglon@wanadoo.fr

Management: Jacques Rols

Built over a smart *brasserie*, the Aiglon is a 3-star plus, spaces are generous and the imperial eagle is much exploited: Empire furniture, even an Empire lift, beside which trickles the stream of a delicious little rockery. In the Empire bar, leather 'books' hide bottles while yellow plush armchairs offer gentle rest. The next delight is the large, light mahogany-panelled breakfast room over the leafy boulevard. Corridors are smartly red and each floor has a 'public' wc — a rare commodity. All rooms have a lobby, walk-in cupboard and furniture made for the Aiglon (beds, chairs, chests-cum-minibar); almost all are large by Paris standards and supremely restful. Walls are yellow or green cloth where furnishings are green and yellow, deep beige where muted multi-coloured prints reign; carpets are soft grey and brown; fine table lamps by Drimmer and watercolours add grace; firm new mattresses guarantee comfort. Bathrooms (all with window) are well-equipped: even the small shower rooms have proper-sized cabins, their light tiling set off by delicate friezes. Many rooms give onto sycamore or acacia-lined avenues, whence most traffic disappears at night, and some survey the green peace of Montparnasse cemetery. The de luxe suite is 'superbly appointed' (the minibar has little columns) and imperially vast. But the reception is by no means haughtily Empire or powerfully Napoleonic. People stay for weeks, come again and become friends of this welcoming family.

Rooms: 38 + 9 suites.
Price: S (shower) 490F; D/TW 610-780F; ST 1030F for 2; ST de luxe 1480F for 1-4.
Breakfast: 40F.
Meals: No.
Metro: Raspail; RER & Orlybus: Denfert Rochereau.
Bus routes: 68 91
Car park: Hotel or Edgar Quinet.

Napoleon's son and heir, nicknamed the "Little Eagle", died in exile at 21 and never carried the Imperial insignia. The previous owner of the hotel was an ardent fan of Napoleon.

Hôtel Raspail Montparnasse

★ ★ ★

203 boulevard Raspail
Paris
75014

Tel: (0)1 43 20 62 86
Fax: (0)1 43 20 50 79
E-mail: hotel.raspail@hol.fr

Management: Madame Christiane Martinent

The frontage is deliciously, authentically 1924, until you step up to those heavy old doors and they spring open... by 1990s magic. 'The best of old and new' is the theme here. Inside, the old-style generosity is again apparent in the big, triple-arched, high-ceilinged Art Deco lobby with its grey plush or black and red bucket chairs, wood-panelled bar and repeated play of squares and curves. The custom-designed bedroom furniture is also 1930s or modern and sits well with unfussy cream or pastel quilts, pretty lamps and an extremely elegant curtain material. Each floor has its own colour scheme: the grey is quiet and relaxing, the ochre is warm and sunny, the blue smacks of boudoirs and powder puffs, and each landing has a 'matching' stained glass window — pleasing recent additions set in the original 1924 framework. Obviously, the higher the price, the larger the room, but even the 'Standard Double' has a decent desk and an armchair while 'Superiors' are most appealing. The suites have double basins, extra chests of drawers and a proper sitting area. Bathrooms are very stylishly white-tiled and colour-friezed and I especially liked the matt white washbasins. Each room is named after one of the artists who were the life and soul of Montparnasse in its heyday, and decorated with an appropriate print; some have the added perk of an Eiffel Tower view. The friendly and efficient welcome is the final flourish. Warning: don't confuse it with the Mercure Raspail Montparnasse two doors down!

Rooms: 38, incl. 2 suites, with bath or shower.
Price: D/TW 730-890F; ST 1160F.
Breakfast: 50F.
Meals: No.
Metro: Vavin, Raspail; RER Port Royal.
Bus routes: 58 68 82 91
Car park: Montparnasse-Raspail.

That statue of Balzac, author of the immense *Comédie Humaine*, by the equally famous sculptor Rodin, shocked contemporaries who saw it as "a madman in his dressing-gown".

Map No: 4

Hôtel Novanox ★ ★ ★

155 boulevard du Montparnasse
Paris
75006

Tel: (0)1 46 33 63 60
Fax: (0)1 43 26 61 72

Management: Bertrand Plasmans

You squeeze past the laurel hedge on the pavement as if to enter some secret country retreat — but it's the Novanox you discover, starting with teak tables and chairs set out for aperitifs or breakfast in this intimate pavement bower. Inside is a 1990s rethink of 50s design in shades of light-hearted yellow and purple: a bar/breakfast room where deep bucket chairs are upholstered with ironic breeze-blowing cherub print, 'photographs' of famous people and typical 50s abstract patterns. You like it or you don't; I do, it is so deeply nostalgic of those post-war years. Lines are cleancut, blond wood furniture is custom-made on conical aluminium legs, lighting is ultra-mod low-voltage pinpoints. Some rooms have a neat corner cupboard or a desk/dressing table whose writing surface lifts up to reveal a mirror, some have a storage alcove round the bed (always an effective use of space); all have a low padded 'actress's' chair, an armchair and reasonable space. Those at the back look onto a quiet side street, while at the front you have the busy boulevard. 2-metre beds are modern but table and bedside lamps keep the 50's theme going. There is also a delightful collection of black and white photographs in plain wooden frames, one per room, of 1950s Paris scenes. Bathrooms are simple and functional, essentially white; one or two baths are fine big relics from the past. If you need a change from flounces and Louis XVI copies, try the Novanox and Bertrand Plasmans' intelligently humorous welcome.

Rooms: 27 with bath or shower.
Price: S/D/TW 680-750F.
Breakfast: Continental plus: 50F + à la carte.
Meals: On request 150-250F.
Metro: Vavin, Raspail; RER Port Royal.
Bus routes: 68 83 91
Car park: Raspail-Montparnasse.

The nearby Grande Chaumière was the name of a dance hall opened by an Englishman called Tinkson in 1788 for Parisians who wanted to do trendy 'English-style' dancing.

Map No: 4

Le Sainte-Beuve ★★★

9 rue Sainte-Beuve
Paris
75006

Tel: (0)1 45 48 20 07
Fax: (0)1 45 48 67 52

Management: Bobette Compagnon

An exceptional address on a quiet street near the Luxembourg gardens — we advise you to book early. Bobette Compagnon has used all her considerable flair (and consulted designer David Hicks) to renovate and redecorate an hotel that was already known and loved during the wilder days of Montparnasse. The immediate atmosphere is of light, restful (but not stuffy) luxury — quiet good taste conveyed in gentle tones and thick furnishings. The new curtains in gold and ivory silk are a superb addition. In winter a log fire burns in the old marble fireplace and clients enjoy taking their drink over to one of the deeply embracing sofas or armchairs to gaze into the flames. The attentive and efficient staff are a vital element in the sense of wellbeing you feel at the Sainte-Beuve. The hotel is small and intimate, and so are the bedrooms. The general tone is Ancient & Modern. Decorated with soft colours and contemporary 'textured' materials, the pastel effect modulated by more colourful chintzes and paisleys, every room has at least one old piece of furniture — a leather-topped desk, an antique dressing-table, a polished *armoire*, old brass lamps — and 18th/19th-century pictures hang in rich old frames. The bathrooms are superbly modern with luxuries such as bathrobes and fine toiletries. Lastly, for the first moments of the day, breakfast is a feast of croissants and brioches from the famous Mulot bakers, homemade jams and freshly-squeezed orange juice.

Rooms: 22 with bathrooms.
Price: S 760F; D1000F; TW 1050F; de luxe 1400-1600F; APT 1810F.
Breakfast: Buffet 90F.
Meals: On request 40-200F.
Metro: Notre-Dame-des-Champs, Vavin; RER Port-Royal.
Bus routes: 48 58 82 89 91 92 94 95 96
Car Park: Montparnasse.

Moral philosopher and literary critic, Sainte Beuve was known for his *bons mots* such as "The historian is a prophet of the past", "So many die before meeting themselves".

Map No: 4

29

Hôtel Le Saint-Grégoire ***
43 rue de l'Abbé Grégoire
Paris
75006

Tel: (0)1 45 48 23 23
Fax: (0)1 45 48 33 95
E-mail: hotel@saintgregoire.com
Net: www.hotelsaintgregoire.com

Management: Michel Bouvier & François de Bené

The utterly Parisian façade of the Saint-Grégoire looks even more 18th-century elegant when compared to the uglies on the other side of the street. Admire its harmonies and enjoy the peace after busy Rue de Rennes. Inside, the elegance is more contemporary: deep comfortable chairs, Indian rugs on fitted carpets and a colour scheme (matching ashtrays) designed by David Hicks. He has conjured up plum, old pink and ginger materials, a red doormat, a brass-ringed half-curtain for privacy, a simple classical fireplace (fires in winter) — and there is a friendly, attentive and intelligent welcome. We found the atmosphere delicious. Sit in the little reading room beside the green mini-patio, listen to gentle classical music, admire the antiques lovingly collected by co-owner Lucie Agaud. In one terrace bedroom, you will find a set of intriguing folding coathooks, in the other, a most unusual thickset writing desk that bears witness to a life of solid serious work. Room sizes vary but every one has a genuinely old piece or two and the mirror frames are lovely. Pinks and browns are favoured, including bathroom marble; bedcovers are mostly bright white piqué, curtains are light florals and the private-home feel is helped by the rugs strewn everywhere. The rooms over the street are larger than the others, some with two windows, though of course it is delightful to have breakfast outside in one of those special terrace rooms. It is small and intimate and remarkably French.

Rooms: 20 (2 with private terrace) & one suite, with bathrooms (1 shower).
Price: ST & T with terrace: 1290-1490F; D/TW Sup. 890-1090F; D Standard 690-890F.
Breakfast: 60F with fresh orange juice & yoghurts.
Meals: They also run La Marlotte restaurant, Rue du Cherche-Midi.
Metro: St Placide, Sèvres-Babylone; RER Luxembourg.
Bus routes: 63 68 84 89 92 94
Car park: Opposite hotel.
Map No: 4

Abbé Grégoire was a revolutionary bishop who proposed ending the feudal Right of Primogeniture (eldest boy takes all) and got France to abolish slavery in 1794.

(some)

Hôtel Ferrandi

* * *

92 rue du Cherche-Midi
Paris
75006

Tel: (0)1 42 22 97 40
Fax: (0)1 45 44 89 97

Management: Madame Lafond

Here we have a delightfully young, cheerful, efficient team — and a drawing room that is a picture-book study of French elegance from two centuries back (apart from the rather awful carpet). This decor is still in vogue today. I particularly liked the white marble fireplace ('log' fire in winter) and the superior club/café feel of the breakfast room with its pretend patio (in fact a wide flowerbed trellissed off from the pedestrian way beyond) that also 'greens' the ground-floor suite. If the flounces seem heavy, there is light relief in Peynet's intelligently naive and suggestive drawings, the 1920s posters and other nostalgia; this marriage of serious and witty is the soul of the place. The suite has a plush *salon* with Regency-stripe paper and a 'Regency' sofabed, heavy curtains, low chairs and a superb bronze-trimmed desk — then you raise your eyes to an unbelievable light fitting with pink and green triffids growing out of it... Venetian. The small blue-and-white bedroom sports a fine cast-iron bedstead and leads to a pink marble bathroom. Other rooms are being redecorated with those quintessentially French Jouy-pattern papers but I also enjoyed the smallest room with its grey hessian walls, thick-weave curtains and arched brass bedhead in an alcove of moulded wood. Furniture is French period style with swagged curtains and canopies — from another century indeed. Now go out and observe the façade: you will see, from the vast spread, why every single room gives onto the street.

Rooms: 42, incl. 1 suite, all with bath or shower.
Price: S/D 580-1280F; TW 680-1280F; ST 1500F.
Breakfast: Continental plus: 65F.
Meals: No.
Metro: Vaneau, St Placide; RER Luxembourg, St Michel-Notre Dame.
Bus routes: 39 95 48 82 68 70
Car park: Hotel or Boucicaut.

Over the road is the little-known museum of the works of Hébert, excellent draughtsman, academic painter of sensitive/sentimental portraits and landscapes. Worth a visit.

Map No: 3

31

Hôtel Normandie Mayet   ***

3 rue Mayet   **Tel:** (0)1 47 83 21 35
Paris   **Fax:** (0)1 40 65 95 78
75006

Management: Monsieur Atmoun

The Normandie has a very pretty Parisian face with its new *marquise* (glass canopy) over the door, green window shades and bright red geraniums; and the little street is blessedly quiet, with just background buzz from the busy boulevard and the fashionable shopping street that is Rue de Sèvres. Inside, you find a surprising and unusual use of space: the bar doubles as reception desk, so you can perch on a stool with a drink while making your booking and chatting with the delightful Stéphanie. This lobby/bar and the adjoining breakfast room are decorated in fine Florentine style and give onto a little well of live greenery and shiny hunting horns behind engraved glass doors. It is all light and charming. The bedrooms are more ordinary in their pale-painted or papered walls, floral upholstery, wooden or padded bedheads. Some are quite small, those with two windows are larger. If you want absolute peace, ask for a courtyard room but they are a little dim, especially on the lower floors. Bathrooms have pale or deep beige tiles and the basics are all there. Refurbishment is planned — corridors, landings and staircases were being redecorated when I visited; Saint Germain des Prés is within walking distance and Monsieur Atmoun is offering our readers very attractive prices: a 10% reduction in High Season (HS) and real bargains in Low Season (LS in 'Price' below) i.e. January, February, March, July and August. And the Italian coffee is excellent.

Rooms: 23 with bath or shower.
Price: S 480F (ASP readers LS 380F);
D/TW 650F (ASP readers LS 450F).
HS less 10% for ASP readers.
Breakfast: 36F.
Meals: No.
Metro: Duroc, Vaneau; RER:
Montparnasse.
Bus routes: 28 39 70 82 87 89 92
Car park: Montparnasse.

For five centuries, the Rue de Sèvres was a country lane leading from Paris to a modest village across the river called... Sèvres. Then porcelain-making fame rose in 1764, never to set.

Map No: 3   (32)

St Germain des Prés – Orsay

50 Frs

Le Madison ★ ★ ★

143 boulevard Saint-Germain
Paris
75006

Tel: (0)1 40 51 60 00
Fax: (0)1 40 51 60 01
E-mail: resa@hotel-madison.com
Net: www.hotel-madison.com

Management: Maryse Burkard

The Madison boasts utterly French elegance in early 1800s style set off by lovely materials from fashionable designers. The hotel is on a set-back tree-lined square, opposite the vastly celebrated *Deux Magots* café; staff have just the right mix of class and 1990s cheerfulness. Its public rooms are luxuriously big and attractive, partly furnished with antiques from the owner's collection. A fine portrait of his mother as a young girl dominates the breakfast area while a powerful cockerel in *porcelaine de Saxe* crows on a pedestal. Through superb hand-made wrought-iron gates, the grand buffet on its tiled C18 sideboard cannot fail to tempt you. Later, the solemn *salon*, with tapestry, pillars and plush sofas, may register your discreet encounters in its silent mirrors. Some bedrooms feel relatively small after these great spaces but all have pleasing modern-smart decor in rich colours and textures with good, coordinated, tiled bathrooms. We liked the larger, double-windowed rooms over the boulevard. No 14 is blue, beige and green with a fine dark green china lamp and shade on a nice old desk and its bathroom is deep red marble. Next door is a smaller room that clients love or loathe — deep raspberry walls, bright yellow bedcovers and curtains, royal blue lamp and chair... vital and provocative! Lastly, the new top-floor suite is a triumph of space, wraparound views of Paris, details like inside shutters, good paintings, shower room AND bathroom. If the Madison is full, try the Bourgogne et Montana.

Rooms: 54 with bath or shower.
Price: S 800-900F; D 1050-1600F; ST 2500F.
Breakfast: Included.
Meals: On request 100-300F.
Metro: St Germain des Prés; RER Châtelet-Les Halles.
Bus routes: 48 58 63 70 86 87 95 96
Car park: St Germain des Prés.

Nowadays, some come to be anonymous, perhaps for deals they can't do in the open at the Ritz, but in an earlier simpler life the Madison housed Camus while he wrote *L'Etranger.*

Hôtel Luxembourg

4 rue de Vaugirard
Paris
75006

* * *

Tel: (0)1 43 25 35 90
Fax: (0)1 43 26 60 84
E-mail: luxhotel@luxembourg.grolier.fr
Net: www.hotel-luxembourg.com

Management: Monsieur Mandin

Just a step from one of Paris's loveliest gardens and within walking distance of all the city's cultural heritage, the Luxembourg is an utterly civilised hotel where your breakfast coffee will come in a silver jug as Mozart wafts gently past. This C17 building was built to house Louix XIV's grooms and is rare in having always been a hostelry. The warmly elegant reception *salon* marries C18 style — including some lovely bits of oriental porcelain — with C20 comfort. And that creeper-climbed, flower-filled, fountain-tinkling patio is perfect for a quiet drink. Rooms have refined touches such as herb essence soaps and more Chinoiserie. They are arranged round the courtyard and are mostly good-sized, the smaller ones being normally let as singles and the lower floors having, obviously, less light. Those that look over the street are efficiently double-glazed. Furnished in the same Louis XVI style with finely painted chairs, stools and mirrors and bedheads that may resemble classical pediments, they are delicately decorated, have adequate storage space and very good tiled bathrooms. Bedcovers are plainly quilted while upholstery and curtains will be flowery or fruity and always expertly coordinated. The soft, quiet atmosphere invites relaxation. Your final discovery will be the tremendous supporting vaults where all that silver is laid for a delicious breakfast. Staff are charming and, final elegance, Monsieur Mandin is happy to offer our readers a half bottle of champagne. As I said, thoroughly civilised.

Rooms: 33 with bathrooms.
Price: S 796-896F; D/TW 912-982F.
(Ask about year-round special rates.)
Breakfast: Included.
Meals: No.
Metro: Odéon; RER Luxembourg.
Bus routes: 21 27 38 82 85
Car park: Rue Soufflot.

The poet Paul Verlaine used to stay here when it was a common lodging house — and walk a few steps to the local café to keep up his deathly *absinthe* habit.

Hôtel Louis II

***

2 rue Saint-Sulpice
Paris
75006

Tel: (0)1 46 33 13 80
Fax: (0)1 46 33 17 29

Management: François Meynant

At the top of this C18 corner building you can sleep under the ancient sloping roof timbers in one of two long flower-papered triple rooms (at the moment, the only two air-conditioned rooms here, but more will come) where crochet bed and table coverings are so fitting. In one there is an old rustic *armoire*, in the other a 1920s free-standing full-length oval mirror. One bathroom has brass taps and a yellow cockleshell basin, the other has an oval bath and burnished copper fittings. The decorator's imagination has been unleashed throughout this charming house, often to dramatic effect (how about pink satin bamboo wallpaper in the loo?), so that even the smallest rooms (some are very tight with little storage) have huge personality. Two rooms have dazzling wraparound *trompe-l'oeil* pictures set into the timber frame by the artist who painted the lift doors (e.g. a wall-mounted safe transforms into a shelf for a great vase of flowers). Every room is different, sheets are floral, bath/shower rooms are small but fully equipped. In the morning you may revel in the slightly worn elegance of the sitting/breakfast room — it is large, lit from two sides and has a fanning beam structure to carry the ceiling round the corner. Gilt-framed mirrors add to the sense of movement; some fine antiques and candelabras complete the picture. You will be enthusiastically welcomed by the friendly new manager and properly cared for: staff, as in their sister hotel, the Globe, treat guests like visiting friends.

Rooms: 22 with bath or shower.
Price: S/D/TW 560-830F; TR 990F; child under 5 free.
Breakfast: Continental plus: 52F.
Meals: No.
Metro: Odéon; RER St Michel-Notre Dame.
Bus routes: 63 87 86 96 58 70
Car park: St Sulpice.

Prince Louis II was the great 17th-century Bourbon Prince de Condé who rebelled against Louis XIV when he was a child king but fought brilliantly for him when he was Sun King.

Map No: 4

Hôtel de l'Odéon

★ ★ ★

13 rue Saint Sulpice
Paris
75006

Tel: (0)1 43 25 70 11
Fax: (0)1 43 29 97 34
E-mail: hotel.de.lodeon@wanadoo.fr
Net: www.hoteldelodeon.com

Management: Monsieur & Madame Pilfert

The Odéon discreetly hides its charms behind a pretty Parisian façade. Enter and discover the most unexpected feast of space, elegance, oak panelling and attention to detail, all set round a delicious green and flowery corner. The Pilferts' collection of antique beds would make any dealer envious — you might have a 4-poster (or two) with tapestry canopy, or a pair of elaborately decorated cast-iron beds, maybe even incorporating a pair of 'statues'. You will also have crochet bedcovers, a nice old mirror, probably a table and chairs and a window onto the narrow street or greenery. Beams abound, while coordinated colour schemes, done with taste and care, convey a sense of quiet traditional comfort; bathrooms are marble. Monsieur has used his ingenuity and sense of architectural volumes to make even the small single rooms feel special (example: two windows cantilevered out over the patio transforming a narrow single room into a real space). Madame makes sure the rooms, all different, are as near perfect as possible. Wherever feasible, those antique bedsteads have been adapted to take extra-wide mattresses. These two really care for your comfort! The generous breakfast can be taken in the 'garden room' that gives onto that lovely little patio with its climbers, creepers, flowers and figurines, or in the comfortable sitting area beside the hand-made, wrought-iron, antique-fitted, glass telephone box — quite a feature. The Odéon is quiet and friendly and there's room to move.

Rooms: 30 with bath or shower.
Price: S 700F; D or TW 790-840F (standard), 930-1050F (superior); TR 1280F; Q 1350F.
Breakfast: 58F.
Meals: No.
Metro: Odéon; RER St Michel-Notre Dame.
Bus routes: 21 27 38 58 82 84 85 89
Car park: St Sulpice.

The secular astronomical Gnomon in St Sulpice catches sunlight from a hole in the wall, projects it onto the brass line inlaid in the floor and thus announces equinoxes and solstices.

Map No: 4

36

Hôtel du Globe ✶✶

15 rue des Quatre-Vents
Paris
75006

Tel: (0)1 46 33 62 69
or (0)1 43 26 35 50
Fax: (0)1 46 33 62 69

Management: Simonne Ressier

Closed in August. Miniature is the word, for the hotel, the rooms, the staircase, the storage — your luggage will need to be pretty miniature too — but huge are the hearts of the small team who run it. They simply adore their little hostelry and want only one thing: that you adore it too. I found it instantly lovable. If you greet the iron man properly, walk up the stairs (there is no lift) without banging your nose on your own reflection or tripping over the thick knobbly carpet, and stop on the first landing, you will find the discreet *Réception* in a sitting room full of furniture and papers and no office equipment at all. You are in someone's house and they welcome you with a smile rather than a form to fill in. All the bedcovers are grandmotherly crochet, there are beams and old stones and four-posters, pink rooms and yellow rooms with little carved *gueridon* tables, tiny folding writing tables, rich-framed mirrors and dozens more personal bits and pieces. No two rooms are alike. The smallest have shower, basin and loo neatly hidden behind doors that would be plain cupboard doors if they weren't hand -painted by a skilful artist. Rooms with baths are larger — one on the ground floor has its own tiny patio — and wherever you sleep you also have your breakfast as there is no breakfast room. Even the drinks list in your bedroom is hand-written. For character, charm and warmth of welcome, the Globe is hard to beat. But do take your earplugs in case you are in a streetside (disco-side) room.

Rooms: 15 with bath or shower.
Price: S/D shower 390-450F;
S/D bath 530F.
Breakfast: 45F.
Meals: No.
Metro: Odéon; RER Cluny-La Sorbonne.
Bus routes: 86 87
Car park: St Sulpice.

In the 17th century, the four winds (Quatre Vents) blew to the four corners of the earth from the round cheeks and delicious lips of four cherubs — on a shop sign.

Map No: 4

37

Le Relais Saint Germain

★ ★ ★ ★

9 carrefour de l'Odéon
Paris
75006

Tel: (0)1 43 29 12 05
Fax: (0)1 46 33 45 30

Management: Alexis Laipsker

Any art buff would stop to peer into the big front windows of this inviting little hotel just because it looks so attractive, unusual and... un-hotelly. A rather daring modern painting sits comfortably in the company of gilt-framed mirrors and old oils, antique furniture and *objets*. Oriental rugs soften marble slabbed floors. Walls are exposed stone or deep orange paint and the woodwork is richly green. A library/sitting area enfolds you in its book-lined cushioned embrace. Altogether smart, peaceful, warmly enticing. In the morning, when the connecting door is unlocked, lucky guests have the adjoining café all to themselves. Laid with cloths and croissants for breakfast, it provides a fine view of the Left Bank walking by. Later in the day, it reverts to being one of the nicest, most authentic small cafés we know in Paris. Bedrooms have beams and more antiques, marble bathrooms, good storage space and, in the higher price ranges, a good deal of space (the superb suite is, of course, especially generous and has its own terrace), while several look out onto Notre Dame. Touches of fantasy include the occasional wooden carving, a pair of scrubbed pine cupboard doors — surprising and deliciously original — and wooden room-dividers looking like iron railings. Throughout, the walls are hung with paintings that have clearly been individually chosen, not bought in lots 'because no-one ever notices'. And YOU will be treated as a valuable individual too.

Rooms: 22 with bath & separate wc.
Price: D 1560F; TW/D 1560-1800F
(4 with kitchen); ST 2050F.
Breakfast: Continental buffet included.
Meals: On request 100-150F.
Metro: Odéon; RER St Michel-Notre Dame.
Bus routes: 27 63 86 87 96
Car parks: Ecole de Médecine, St Germain des Prés, St Sulpice.

We associate *odeon* with cinemas and the Paris Odéon has been a theatre since it was built in 1818. The Greek 'odeion' was in fact a theatre for musical or dramatic performances.

Map No: 4

(38)

 (some)

Hôtel Saint André des Arts ★★

66 rue Saint-André-des-Arts
Paris
75006

Tel: (0)1 43 26 96 16
Fax: (0)1 43 29 73 34
E-mail: hsaintand@minitel.net

Management: Monsieur Legoubin

The old shop front of this supremely relaxed, welcoming and low-cost hotel beside the bustling Place St André des Arts has been known and loved by academics and intellectuals for years. They push the door onto a row of old choir stalls, a half-timbered ground floor, a listed staircase and a former philosphy teacher. He prefers hotel-keeping to teaching: the students come of their own accord and are HAPPY to talk *philo...* in all simplicity. Many rooms have been redecorated, mattresses are new, the free-standing shower cabins are being replaced by white and yellow tiled shower rooms and the coconut matting wall coverings are giving way to plain paint in the corridors. But nothing can ever hide how they twist and turn, revealing the way the building has always been articulated round the courtyard. One room is even reached by crossing a balcony. Ceilings are sometimes immensely high with fine great windows to match, beams, timbers, old stone walls — all the signs of great age and lasting quality. Japanese grass paper in various shades on the walls, 'ethnic' print curtains, practical basic furniture in Rustic French Antique style, made especially in Montpellier. Breakfast is in the reception area at a wonderful great 'folding' table set on a *trompe-l'œil* black and white floor that was laid 200 years ago. The neighbourhood is lively, the music sometimes noisy and nocturnal, the atmosphere stimulating. If you feel you would like to join in, book early — it's often full.

Rooms: 31 with bath or shower.
Price: Incl. breakfast D 480F;
TW 520F; TR 590F; Q 650F.
Breakfast: Included in price.
Meals: No.
Metro: Odéon; RER St Michel-Notre Dame.
Bus routes: 63 70 86 87 96
Car park: Rue Mazarine.

'Arts' really means 'arcs': this was the arms merchants' district. Two muskets discovered on the old hotel reception wall betray the origins of the C16 house.

Map No: 4

Hôtel de Nesle

7 rue de Nesle   **Tel:** (0)1 43 54 62 41
Paris
75006

Management: Madame Busillet & David Busillet

This is a backpackers' hostel *extraordinaire*, NOT a hotel for those needing clean towels every day, loads of storage and all quiet by 10.30 pm. There is no other hotel like it and no other owner like Madame Renée, as everyone calls the good-looking matron who rules her lively young visitors with voice, gesture and *bonhomie*. With its old bits of furniture and innumerable bunches of dried flowers, the reception area communicates a carefree atmosphere while a fine collection of old Larousses adds a serious touch. Then, first floor, first surprise: a big garden, with roses, apricot trees and a pond — half the rooms give onto it. The second surprise is in your room: the walls carry bright frescoes designed to initiate foreigners into the history of France. Try 'Afrique' for French explorers, mosquito-netted bed and African objects, 'Sahara' for a private open patio with a genuine (miniature) hammam, or 'Ancienne' for old photographs and lace. All individually furnished with *brocante* and pretty whatnots, mirrors, soft modern colours and great charm, the rooms are spotlessly clean and have good firm mattresses. BUT, even if the price suits your pocket and the old beams please your eye, you may find the facilities and services too scant for your comfort: virtually no storage, one shower (magnificent in dark green marble with romantic broken column) for 10 rooms and NO advance booking. Ring or come in the morning for the evening... and enjoy the warm friendliness. No credit cards either.

Rooms: 10 with shower & wc; 10 with basin, sharing one shower & 4 wc's.
Price: D with basin 275F; D with shower & wc 350-450F.
Breakfast: 25F.
Meals: No.
Metro: Odéon; RER St Michel-Notre Dame.
Bus routes: 58 63 70 86 87 96
Car park: Rue Mazarine.

The Tower of Nesle was (in)famous for housing princesses who seduced and "used" handsome young men then threw them into the river to conceal their own depravities.

Map No: 4   40

Welcome Hôtel ★ ★

66 rue de Seine **Tel:** (0)1 46 34 24 80
Paris **Fax:** (0)1 40 46 81 59
75006

Management: Monsieur Henneveux, Perrine Henneveux

It is well-named — the ground-floor reception area is tiny but the smile that greets you is big and genuine: you could be old friends coming for a weekend. The Welcome is on the corner of Rue de Seine and Boulevard St Germain — in the middle of one of the trendiest parts of Paris offering both the delightfully popular Rue de Buci street market and the legendary cafés *Flore* and *Deux Magots*. This double background rubs off on the Welcome: it has that comfortable atmosphere created by a natural and unpretentious attitude to life and people. On the first floor is the timbered tapestried *salon* which looks down onto the bustle below. The big table with its high-backed cane chairs can take a dozen or so for breakfast, otherwise you breakfast in your room. Most rooms are small, of course, and all give onto one or other of the streets so you will be grateful for efficient double-glazing. The decor varies — quite a lot — and some parts need freshening up, just like an old family country house, but it has all the charm of that kind of home. Top-floor rooms have sloping ceilings and beams: one is reached through the half-timbered bathroom! A couple have great views across the treetops and the boulevard; you may find blue hessian walls with an Andean bedcover, or eau-de-nil walls and a tapestry bed, or orange cloth walls and a blue/orange bed and little old pieces of furniture. Each room is different — the best have two windows and more space — and personality is palpable throughout.

Rooms: 30 with bath or shower.
Price: S 495-605F; D shower 605F;
TW bath 655F.
Breakfast: 40F + à la carte.
Meals: No.
Metro: St Germain des Prés, Mabillon, Odéon; RER St Michel-Notre Dame.
Bus routes: 39 48 58 63 70 86 87 95
Car park: St Germain des Prés, St Sulpice.

The oldest part of the Rue de Seine dates back to 1489 when it carried supplies from the river port to the wealthy Abbey of St Germain which owned this whole area.

Map No: 4

41

Hôtel de Seine ★★★

52 rue de Seine
Paris
75006

Tel: (0)1 46 34 22 80
Fax: (0)1 46 34 04 74

Management: Monsieur Henneveux, Perrine Henneveux

Underneath the arches, through the big wooden doors, and you enter what once was, and still feels like, a private mansion; the welcome from the delightful staff adds to this impression. There are two antique-furnished, richly-decorated, thick-carpeted, bronze-lit *salons* off the hallway, fresh flowers, space and deep quiet. One *salon* is the breakfast room, presided over by a delicate little Pan. In deference to guests' different tastes, it has one large table for the sociable and several small tables for the less so. The walls are clothed in Florentine-style cloth, the chairs are blue-upholstered and studded, the corners prettily dressed with old quarter-circle cupboards. Reached along rich pink and turquoise corridors, the bedrooms have just as much class with their strong, complementary colour schemes — mustard and blue, or red and beige, or deep pink and lettuce green — their furniture that may be gently painted Louis XVI or highly polished, cane-seated Directoire and, again, that sense of being part of someone's home, not an anonymous hotel. One room displays a rather daring use of black paint and gilt edging in honour of the C19 craze for all things Far Eastern; others are laid out in original ways dictated by the old architecture. The elegant marble bathrooms have lots of mirrors and heated towel rails and the higher floors naturally offer C18 timbers and the occasional balcony for rooftop views or birds-eye vistas of fine Parisian façades. A good place to stay.

Rooms: 30 with bath or shower.
Price: S 695F; D 820F; TW 890F;
de luxe 980F.
Breakfast: 50F + à la carte.
Meals: No.
Metro: St Germain des Prés, Mabillon, Odéon; RER St Michel-Notre Dame.
Bus routes: 39 48 58 63 70 86 87 95
Car park: Mazarine.

Francis Ford Coppola used to have reels of film delivered openly to the Crillon (Paris's most exclusive palace hotel) while he stayed incognito at the simple Seine.

Map No: 4

(some)

Hôtel des Deux Continents   * * *

25 rue Jacob   **Tel:** (0)1 43 26 72 46
Paris   **Fax:** (0)1 43 25 67 80
75006   **Net:** www.france-hotel-guide.com/h75006continent

Management: Monsieur Henneveux, Perrine Henneveux

Hotels, interior decorators and antique shops jostle for space here so don't miss the discreet entrance to the Deux Continents tucked into its three ancient, listed buildings. The ground-floor sitting and breakfast rooms are full of beams, heavy gilt-framed mirrors, old views of Paris, elegant draperies and old furniture. The atmosphere is lightened at the front by the big window onto the street and at the back by a little patio. Here Venus stands shyly among the green stuff and breakfast tables are laid with fine white cloths and bright china against a green and gold backdrop. The geography of the hotel changes interestingly as you move inwards; two buildings look onto quiet inner courtyards; the front building has the larger but noisier rooms. They are done in contemporary-classic style with lots of material — on walls, bedheads, covers, curtains, pelmets, the odd canopy — in occasionally surprising mixtures of colours and patterns; but it all 'works', as do the discreet desks, curly bronze light fittings and pretty old mirrors. The smallest (cheapest) rooms are in the last building (two storeys, no lift) — they are utterly quiet, equally charming and have the advantage of air conditioning. Some rooms have rooftop views, some look onto flowered terraces. Bath and shower rooms vary in size too; some are tiled, some marble, some more recently refurbished than others — it all takes time. The whole place has lots of personality, the staff are young and welcoming and you are ideally placed for St Germain des Prés.

Rooms: 41 with bath or shower.
Price: S/D shower 715-895F;
D/TW bath 765-835F; TR 1040F.
Breakfast: 50F + à la carte.
Meals: No.
Metro: St Germain des Prés; RER St
Michel-Notre Dame.
Bus routes: 39 48 63 86 95
Car park: St Germain des Prés.

Which two continents? The Old World and the New. In 1783 America and Great Britain signed the Treaty of Independence in a house just a few blocks down from here.

Map No: 4

Hôtel des Marronniers

21 rue Jacob
Paris
75006

* * *

Tel: (0)1 43 25 30 60
Fax: (0)1 40 46 83 56

Management: Monsieur Henneveux, Perrine Henneveux

With its real garden, this is another of the Henneveux 'private mansion' hotels just behind St Germain des Prés. The entrance through the great arch and across the courtyard (notice the ineffably Parisian *concierge's* lodge on the left) promises peace but does not prepare you for what you find. There is a grandiose Empire-style lobby/*salon*, all ruched drapes and gilt frames, a delicious conservatory where red-cushioned cast-iron garden chairs and marble-topped bistro tables invite you to sit under the fruit-and-leaf 'chandeliers' and, at last, a shrubby garden with more tables and chairs. A privilege indeed. Room sizes vary: most are smallish but they all give onto the garden or the front courtyard so no need for double glazing. From the top floor you may see higgledy-piggledy rooftops or the bell tower of St Germain; from all rooms you will hear nostalgic chimes. The decor is based on coordinated/contrasted materials (walls, curtains, canopies, beds), variously bright floral prints or Regency stripes serving as a backdrop to an antique desk, for example, a carved country *armoire* or a pair of lemon-tree spray light fittings. There is lots of character here. Bathrooms have all been recently renovated and are most attractive, be they grey and ginger marble or white tiles with an original tropical island 'picture', or simply a bright floral frieze. After so much light, the basement breakfast room is in soft, dark contrast for cool winter mornings. Or hie ye to the conservatory.

Rooms: 37 with bath or shower.
Price: S shower 560F; D 755-855F;
TW 805-1005F; TR 960-1080F.
Breakfast: 50F + à la carte.
Meals: No.
Metro: St Germain des Prés;
RER St Michel-Notre Dame.
Bus routes: 39 48 63 86 95
Car park: St Germain des Prés.

Strangely, this street bears Jacob's name because Queen Margot, Catholic wife of (originally) Protestant King Henri IV built a shrine to the Jewish patriarch here.

Map No: 4

(44)

L'Hôtel ★★★★

13 rue des Beaux Arts
Paris
75006

Tel: (0)1 44 01 99 00
Fax: (0)1 43 25 64 81

Management: Alain-Philippe Feutré

Astonishing! Dare I say unique? Beyond the little doorway and hall with book-lined *salon* on one side and reception-study on the other, we see right through to a classical stone fountain at the back of a long indoor garden. Then, as we walk towards the tinkling water, our eyes are drawn up, up, up past marble pilasters and five circular medallioned galleries to the light. All rooms give onto this well, otherwise they are daringly different. Guy-Louis Duboucheron's decorating talent went to rich plush and brocade wall coverings and curtains, elaborate bronze lamp-holders, Chinese lacquer and a generally heavy Victorian look. Here, brilliantly reconstituted, is the room where Oscar Wilde died; and music-hall star Mistinguett's outrageously glamorous bedroom where it's all done with mirrors (illustrated). The larger top-floor apartment is sumptuous with its terrace view, real dining room, Persian rugged *salon* and green marble bathroom. The other is more intimately French in green and blue Genoa velvet with a bijou ginger and grey marble bathroom. All furniture, lamps, pictures and *objets* are genuine — this is a place for true connoisseurs who know that no amount of money can replace one of a pair of original vases. Rooms are huge in character, small in size; some bathrooms are very small. The bar and great garden space, now barrel-roofed with 'Renaissance' coffering, has a real tree trunk, big plants, splendid great steel birds, a piano and a relaxed atmosphere round the lovely old fountain.

Rooms: 27, incl. 2 apartments, all with bath or shower.
Price: D shower 600-1000F; D bath 1500-2500F; TW shower 850-1400F; TW bath 1000-1800F; APT 1700-3600F.
Breakfast: 100F.
Meals: On request 50F and upwards.
Metro: St Germain des Prés; RER St Michel-Notre Dame, Châtelet-Les Halles.
Bus routes: 39 48 95
Car park: Rue Mazarine.
Map No: 4

The École des Beaux Arts is famous with some for the innumerable Great Men of Art and Architecture it has produced since 1648... and with others for its outrageous student rag days.

Hôtel de l'Académie   * * *

32 rue des Saints Pères
Paris
75006

Tel: (0)1 45 49 80 00
Toll-free USA: 1 800 246 0041
Fax: (0)1 45 49 80 10
E-mail: AAAcademie@aol.com

Management: Pierre Chekroun

When you push the door into this white-rendered, window-boxed building, you leave a street bustling with Parisian traffic and beautiful people for a cool, quiet haven. Young, relaxed staff welcome you to the old-fashioned atmosphere of an antique-furnished hotel where Olde France seems very present. With contemporary expectations in mind, rooms are regularly refurbished: paintwork is impeccable, bedding new, bathrooms spotless marble — nothing has time to get worn or stale. I found the plain-painted walls a restful way of setting off the old beams and choice pieces such as a vast two-layered, gilt-framed oval mirror or a nice old ormulu Louis XV chest with its elaborate bronze fittings. A couple of little kidney-shaped bedside tables were a delight. The ground-floor breakfast room is cleverly arranged, incorporating an inner lightwell and playing with mirrors and infinite depths — the two round tables set between two mirrors and seductively close to the Junoesque figure are said to be very popular. You can have a caterer dinner here too if you wish. Bedrooms and bathrooms are biggish, by Paris standards, and storage space has been carefully planned. The feel is of friendly, smiling yet professional people doing their best to make sure you return. It's good value for money and, to cap that, Monsieur Chekroun offers our readers a free bottle of red (Haut Médoc or Saint Emilion) or white (Sancerre or Chablis) wine... so take this book with you.

Rooms: 29 D/TW with bath; 5 suites with whirlpool bath.
Price: D/TW 490-990F; ST 990-1590F.
Breakfast: Full buffet 60F.
Meals: On request 150F.
Metro: St Germain des Prés; RER Musée d'Orsay.
Bus routes: 48 63 86 95
Car park: Hotel car park.

Antonio Machado, one of Spain's greatest modern poets, lived here for some of his political exile in the 1930s. There may be a plaque up by the time you arrive.

Hôtel de l'Université ★ ★ ★
22 rue de l'Université
Paris
75007

Tel: (0)1 42 61 09 39
Fax: (0)1 42 60 40 84
E-mail: hoteldeluniversite@minitel.net

Management: Madame Bergmann &
Monsieur Teissedre

(some)

In a city where a square metre is worth a small fortune, the double-doored entrance, the vista through to the green patio, the split-level, timber-framed sitting room, the wide shallow staircase leading naturally to high-ceilinged bedrooms are a privilege and even the smaller rooms (some are only given as singles) are pretty, with neat little shower or bathrooms. It is decorated like a grand embracing home with items that Madame Bergmann has ferretted out in flea markets and antique shops over the years. There are tapestries (or bits of them) in the right places, old prints in old frames ("Authentic or not at all — don't hold with copies" she says), wooden statues, pieces of furniture from all periods. The breakfast room gives onto the leafy patio. You eat at a long marble bistro table, seated on a fine long black velvet bench, or *chez vous* under the honeysuckle if you have taken one of the stunning terrace rooms. Most rooms have writing table or armchair or sofa — or all three — and white bedcovers that don't steal your attention away from the best pieces. Some have the original C18 panelling and built-in cupboards and more oak is being used for cornices and dados for an ever richer effect. All have good bathrooms, lots of marble and the right accessories. But enjoy the views too: over the Ministry of Commerce with its huge neo-classical portico and the Ecole Nationale d'Administration, academic cradle of great careers — innumerable senior civil servants, ministers and even Presidents of the Republic.

Rooms: 27, inc. 2 with terrace, all with bath or shower.
Price: S 500-750F; D/TW 850-1200F; TR 1000-1500F.
Breakfast: Continental plus: 50F & à la carte.
Meals: Light meals 50-150F.
Metro: St Germain des Prés; RER Musée d'Orsay.
Bus routes: 24 27 39 48 63 68 69 70 87 95
Car park: Montalembert.

In the 12th century, the monks of St Germain Abbey used to have their ice house in the powerfully vaulted basement of this hotel, where there is now a superb meeting room for guests.

Hôtel de Lille ★★
40 rue de Lille
Paris
75007

Tel: (0)1 42 61 29 09
Fax: (0)1 42 61 53 97
E-mail: hotel-de-lille@wanadoo.fr

Management: Michel Margouilla

Small, simple, cleancut, impeccably maintained — the Lille is a bargain in this smart antique-shopping neighbourhood. On a quiet street behind the Seine embankment, it is half way between the cafés of St Germain des Prés, where the fun-loving crowd congregates, and the intense culture trip to the Orsay Museum. The strictness of the lobby's 1930s style with its yellow walls, green bucket armchairs, black wood-trimmed desk and bar, is softened by big packets of greenery by the window and in the minuscule lightwell. And when you go down to breakfast, you enter another universe. The vast stone vaults feel ancient indeed and the garden-style rattan furniture with soft upholstery makes this a tempting sitting and eating area. Bedrooms are to scale: small, compact, furnished either with a 1930s veneered cupboard or desk or with cane-and-bamboo pieces. The white walls are a good foil to the well-coordinated rich-coloured prints of curtains, quilts and stool cushions and top-floor rooms have beams for an even cosier atmosphere. In one room everything, including the back wall, is done in the same print of a collection of Chinamen at a hot-air balloon launch — a humorous touch. Bathrooms are amazingly good for 20 years old! Marie-José, the delightful receptionist, and the owner himself are friendly and relaxed, but he also keeps an eagle eye on the state of your quilt and the bathroom tiles. However, refurbishment is planned and hair dryers are to be installed in 1999.

Rooms: 20 with bath or shower.
Price: S 520F; D/TW standard 610F; D/TW superior 620-800F.
Breakfast: Included.
Meals: No.
Metro: Rue du Bac, St Germain des Prés, Tuileries; RER Orsay.
Bus routes: 48 49 68 69 95
Car park: Montalembert.

You may remember the Lille from your student days when washing facilities were communal, the price was 30F per night and the walls were made of cork!

Map No: 4

Hôtel Bersoly's Saint Germain   ***

28 rue de Lille   **Tel:** (0)1 42 60 73 79
Paris   **Fax:** (0)1 49 27 05 55
75007

Management: Mademoiselle Carbonnaux

Closed in August. Guests are welcomed here as friends. How could they be otherwise in such a tiny, intimate house? Sylvie Carbonnaux is charming and unflappable with a relaxed approach that instantly puts you at ease. Built in the 1600s as a convent, the house has the patina of a genuine antique, from the beautiful irregular paving stones of the lobby to the slim elegance of the listed banisters. Rather than the little lift, take the stairs and enjoy the Impressionist copies that grace the landings in their ornate frames. The rooms, each hung with a particular painter's work, recall the original cell dimensions imposed upon the nuns — they are very small, with old beams and large modern ceiling fans (and air conditioning), but all accommodate a nice old piece of furniture or two as well as tea-making equipment. Bathrooms are snug and pretty, each with a different tiling motif. Furnishings are soft shades of pink and yellow or, unexpectedly, large floral designs that set off old wardrobes. A suite of 2 communicating rooms can be had on each floor. Top-floor rooms have sloping ceilings and more space (room for a couple of armchairs); 'Pissaro's' bath sits inside the timber frame(!) and 'Degas's' bathroom is up a private stair. On the ground floor, 'Picasso' is reached through its own tiny courtyard with garden furniture and a great sense of privacy. To reach the finely vaulted breakfast rooms in the basement you go past the attractive little bar with promises of evening aperitifs.

Rooms: 16 with shower or bath.
Price: S/D 600-700F; TW 750F.
1 Nov-31 Mar: same price including breakfast.
Breakfast: 50F (included in low season) + à la carte.
Meals: Caterer-delivered 60-150F.
Metro: St Germain des Prés, Rue du Bac; RER Musée d'Orsay.
Bus routes: 24 27 39 48 63 68 69 86 87 95
Car park: Hotel or Montalembert.

The brave citizens of Lille are commemorated here for resisting the Austrians in 1792 when all the crowned heads of Europe ganged up on the French Revolution.

Map No: 4   (49)

Hôtel Verneuil ★★★

8 rue de Verneuil
Paris
75007

Tel: (0)1 42 60 82 14
Fax: (0)1 42 61 40 38
E-mail: verneuil@cybercable.fr
Net: www.francehotelsguide

Management: Sylvie de Lattre

When she took over the Verneuil, Sylvie de Lattre's intention was to make her guests feel as at home as in a private house; she has definitely achieved her aim. The welcoming *salon* is like a country drawing room furnished with pieces of family history, tempting books and chairs to curl up in; the smallish bedrooms (some only just make the 3-star size rules), all different, have painted beams or carved bedheads or a canopied bed or a pilastered frame against the wall. Some things were inherited and adapted, like the successfully overpainted wall cloth with its *trompe-l'œil* panels. Some are personal possessions; some, such as the fascinating variety of engravings, portraits and drawings, were chosen room by room. Finally, your charming young hostess has such a natural sense of welcome that you are instantly at ease. The decor is one of understated strength, bedcovers are thick white piqué, walls have definite, original designs for a lively effect (see illustration) or plain pastels to set off other features. Firm-mattressed beds are high enough for suitcases to hide under and windows are clothed in fine linen nets as well as beautiful coordinated curtains. One 'regular' room is like a little red box, warm and intimate, reached by walking under a massive main C17 beam. Bathrooms are small but complete and the vaulted basement breakfast room pleasant with rustic tables, red upholstered chairs and fine white china. Quietly classy, this is a delicious find between St Germain and the river.

Rooms: 26 with bathrooms.
Price: S 650F; D 700-750; TW 800F; de luxe 950F.
Breakfast: Continental buffet 50F + à la carte.
Meals: On request 100F.
Metro: St Germain des Prés, Rue du Bac; RER Orsay, St Michel-Notre Dame.
Bus routes: 39 48 68 69 73 95
Car park: St Germain des Prés.

The Duke of Verneuil's Marchioness mother got the title, plus a small fortune, from King Henri IV, father of her illegitimate son, but never the crown he'd promised.

Map No: 4

(some)

Hôtel Bourgogne et Montana ***

3 rue de Bourgogne
Paris
75007

Tel: (0)1 45 51 20 22
Fax: (0)1 45 56 11 98
E-mail: bourgogne-montana.com

Management: Martine Monney

In a very smart area where important people (MPs) dash about in the daytime, it is a delicious relief to enter the also-smart Bourgogne; the staff here only take themselves half seriously, the half required to do their job properly. The other half is all light-hearted attentive welcome. The MP theme is used throughout, with wicked cartoon portraits of real individuals — from an earlier generation. We love the combination of efficiency and wit — the French at their best. Beyond the lobby is the famous rotunda with its pink pilasters, mirrors and unreal roundness under a translucent ceiling, the dark-panelled, leather-chaired *salon* and the deeply tempting breakfast room, full of light and the most sinful buffet (included in the price). Two floors are air-conditioned, the rest are being done; the lift is a wonder of pre-war oak panels and ironwork. The newly renovated floors have dado panelling in the same wood and even richer, thicker upholstery than before. It IS a luxy hotel, especially the big new apartment with its supremely stylish white, grey and pale yellow colour scheme, two bathrooms and huge draped bed. Suites and 'superior' rooms have space and antique furniture, lovely china lamps, thick quilted upholstery and some (Nos 57 and 67) extraordinary bathrooms. The smaller rooms, cheaper yet still extremely comfortable, have the same harmonious mix'n match colours and patterns and perfectly good marble and tile bathrooms. And there's that feast for breakfast. If the hotel is full, try the Madison.

Rooms: 27 & 6 apartments/junior suites with bath or shower.
Price: S 900-1730F; D or ST 1070-1800F.
Breakfast: Buffet included.
Meals: No.
Metro: Assemblée Nationale, Invalides; RER + Air France bus: Invalides.
Bus routes: 93 83 63
Car park: Invalides.

The Duc de Bourgogne in question, father of Louis XV, once famously told his Sun King of a grandfather, Louis XIV : "A king is made for his subjects, not subjects for their king".

Map No: 1 & 3

Invalides – Eiffel Tower

Hôtel de la Tulipe ★★

33 rue Malar
Paris
75007

Tel: (0)1 45 51 67 21
Fax: (0)1 47 53 96 37
Net: www.paris.com/TULIPE

Management: Monsieur &
Madame Fortuit

The Tulipe is as delightful as ever, your hosts are easy, friendly, intelligent and a pleasure to meet. A small intimate hotel, it was once a convent and has rooms set around the green, honeysuckled, cobbled courtyard (where you may sit) or over the quiet street; some have windows onto both. Most rooms seem small but they all represent at least two cells... and two are in the former chapel. In fact, this has been an hotel since the influx of visitors to the *Exposition Universelle* in 1900. There are beams and old stone walls, some newly yellow-sponged walls with deep red carpets, simple pine or cane furniture (though the peacock-tail bedhead and chair don't qualify as simple), patchwork bedcovers and white curtains, or bright Provençal prints and cream covers. Many of the bath/shower rooms have very fitting blue-pattern, country-style tiling; the renovated ones have bright sunflower-yellow paint. The one room without a wc has its own across the landing. Two new rooms, one equipped for disabled guests, lead directly off the patio and have a specially peaceful and connected feel because of this. The new breakfast/tea room is utterly charming with its pale stone tiles, blond timbers, slim-legged conservatory furniture and interesting paintings... and croissants fresh each day from the local bakery. Above all, together with the unpretentiousness of the Fortuit family and their hotel we remember their smiles and relaxed manner and so, most certainly, will you.

Rooms: 22 with shower or bath.
Price: S 498F; D 500-650F.
Breakfast: 45F with cheese and baker's croissants.
Meals: Daytime snacks in 'tea room'.
Metro & RER: Invalides, Pont de l'Alma.
Bus routes: 49 63 69 80 92
Car park: Rue Malar.

"Before the war, rue Malar was full of little shops — a button-mender (for tiny cloth-covered buttons), a seller of wine by the glass, all killed by the supermarkets." A former tenant, 60 years on.

Map No: 1

Hôtel du Palais Bourbon ★★
49 rue de Bourgogne
Paris
75007

Tel: (0)1 44 11 30 70
Fax: (0)1 45 55 20 21
E-mail: htlbourbon@aol.com

Management: Thierry Claudon

In a district of fine old mansions — now occupied by civil servants, of course — nothing prepares you for the volumes of the hotel that spreads and rambles here, least of all the small, unassuming doorway — don't miss it! You will be greeted by the delightful South American Rafael, or Monsieur, or Madame Mère. The atmosphere is comfortably casual and loyal staff stay for years — always a good sign. The lobby has a terrifically high, beamed ceiling, white walls, a warm brick desk and five attractive green-cushioned cane armchairs. Then you pass through into the depths and discover that it feels like a quiet country house, occupying two connecting buildings and full of secret spaces. Staircases announce their C18 origins: they are gently unsteep; all the rooms are different, those on the lower floors being unusually big for two Parisian stars. The top-floor doubles have great character with their sloping ceilings and beams and the little singles are excellent value. The decor is quiet and unprovocative, based on soft pastels in peachy paint or mild stripes or delicate florals while carpets are mostly beige. Each room has an individual touch, be it an oriental rug or a country antique and the essential pieces of furniture — beds, wardrobes, desk units — are custom-made in Brittany. Those bathrooms that have been recently renovated are simple and excellent with their white tiling and pretty friezes, the taps and fittings are ultra-modern, the space generous.

Rooms: 32 with bath or shower (exc. 4 singles sharing).
Price: S 300-480F; D/TW 580F; TR 672F; Q 740F.
Breakfast: Included.
Meals: No.
Metro: Invalides, Varenne, Assemblée Nationale; RER Invalides.
Bus routes: 24 63 69 73 83 84 94
Car park: Invalides.

The 'Bourbon Palace' was seized from its aristocratic owners in 1790 to become the 'House of the Revolution' and has housed the National Assembly since the Restoration.

Eiffel Park Hôtel

17bis rue Amélie
Paris
75007

***

Tel: (0)1 45 55 10 01
Fax: (0)1 47 05 28 68

Management: Françoise Testard

An example of how to make cold stone human, the Eiffel Park was built as a cleancut, all-shiny, all-hygienic businessmen's hotel — and had a change of heart. The softening process is a great success, relying on lots of Asian furniture and *objets*. The high yellow hall is now dressed with a big oriental rug on its granite floor, colonial-style rattan armchairs and daybed round a wonderful 'coffee' table made from a pair of Indian shutters, and a gigantic Provençal urn with matching sunflowers. Go through a finely carved Indian garden doorway to the soft-smart bar and sitting area then to the breakfast room with its high-tech tables and chairs and patio extension (open in summer, canvassed and heated in winter). It all fits very well. In each bedroom you find pieces of rustic-looking Far-Eastern furniture — coat stands, little chests, bedside tables, highly polished or hand-painted to match the colour scheme. This may be blue and sunny gold or vibrant pink and red, for example. Rooms are by no means huge but there are some quirky shapes and window angles which give a sense of more space. The bathrooms have superbly classic white tiles and fittings and four communicating apartments can be 'created'. Last, but far from least, there is a wonderful roof terrace where grapes grow on vines, lavender flowers and you can have summer breakfast while gazing across the roofscape. A lively, friendly welcome completes the picture. ASP readers who stay three nights get their third breakfast free!

Rooms: 36 with bath.
Price: S 550-650F; D/TW600-750F; de luxe 940F.
Breakfast: Buffet 55F. Free your third morning.
Meals: No.
Metro: La Tour Maubourg; RER+Air France bus: Invalides.
Bus routes: 28 49 63 69
Car park: Invalides.

You can discover fascinatingly natural carpets, covers and draperies handmade by Moroccan desert peoples at 'Thanakra' just round the corner in Rue de Grenelle.

Map No: 3

Hôtel du Champ de Mars ★★

7 rue du Champ de Mars
Paris
75007

Tel: (0)1 45 51 52 30
Fax: (0)1 45 51 64 36
E-mail: stg@club-internet.fr
Net: www.adx.fr/HOTEL-DU-CHAMP-DE-MARS

Management: Françoise & Stéphane Gourdal

The harmonious architect-designed frontage lets you into a light and welcoming reception/sitting area where a few bright-striped button armchairs beckon. While you are being warmly greeted by Françoise or Stéphane, Chipie the French spaniel may offer a friendly wag. The padded, orange-clothed chairs in the rustic-walled basement breakfast room, where gentle classical music can be heard, are also very appealing. The building grows round two tiny green-planted courtyards and your room, named after a flower, is decorated in yellow on blue or... blue on yellow, depending on which side of the building it is on, and the same theme is used very gently on the stairs and landings. It is all done with delightful coordinated checks and florals; wallpapers are smartly but discreetly striped and fine botanical prints adorn the walls. There is a nice piece of furniture in each room; lighting is good and, although the rooms are a bit small, storage is definitely adequate and so are the well-renovated bathrooms. The whole atmosphere is one of family intimacy and peaceful backwaters — almost a country house feel. But you will find excitement enough at the famous street market in nearby Rue Cler, and the narrow leafy paths of the Champ de Mars are at the end of the street. The Eiffel Tower is at the bottom of this garden. Public transport to all parts of Paris is excellent too. Very good value.

Rooms: 25 with bath or shower.
Price: S 355-385F; D 360-420F;
TR 505F.
Breakfast: 35F.
Meals: No.
Metro: Ecole Militaire; RER Invalides,
Pont de l'Alma.
Bus routes: 28 49 80 82 92
Car park: Ecole Militaire.

No 33 in this street is an Art Nouveau feast of stone and wrought-iron leaves, tendrils, pistils and curlicues leaping skywards past a glass canopy that manages to make straight panels look curvy.

Map No: 3

Hôtel Relais Bosquet-Tour Eiffel ★★★

19 rue du Champ de Mars
Paris
75007

Tel: (0)1 47 05 25 45
Fax: (0)1 45 55 08 24
E-mail: webmaster@relais-bosquet.com
Net: www.relais-bosquet.com

Management: Dora & Philippe Hervois

The delight on entering this hotel is even greater for its unexpectedness — beyond the unprepossessing doorway lies a big, colourful, cushioned sitting room, adorned with two lovely silk-screen prints, plus two attractive connecting breakfast rooms (one for smokers). There is, too, a long, Persian-rugged vista past twin patios where garden furniture, magnolia and creepers promise a cool resting place. 23 rooms are on one or other side of this courtyard while 17 look onto the street. The sense of space and peace comes with a remarkable sense of service. The people at reception, be they owners or staff, are quietly attentive; each room has a tea-making kit, iron and ironing board, four pillows, modem socket and masses of coat hangers. The careful decor is based on either the red, the blue or the green theme, with really pretty prints for curtains and head cushions, white quilted bedcovers, one or two big upholstered stools as suitcase racks and a fine modern white bathroom (double basins in 'Superior' rooms) where the trim reflects the room's colour scheme. Bedrooms and bathrooms all have *space*, the furniture is good modern trad, all beds are zippable twin doubles (extra long in 'Superiors') and the lighting is just right. Every print or engraving has been chosen for its particular character and framed accordingly. The occasional antique is an added personal touch and staff will organise baby-sitting or secretarial workers for you. A most likeable hotel two minutes from the Eiffel Tower.

Rooms: 40 with bathrooms.
Price: S 550-800F; D/TW 650-900F; extra bed 100F.
Breakfast: Generous continental 57F + à la carte.
Meals: No.
Metro: Ecole Militaire; RER Pont de l'Alma.
Bus routes: 28 49 82 80 92
Car park: Ask at hotel.

General Bosquet saved the English army fighting under Lord Cardigan at Inkerman (Crimea) and was made Field Marshal AND Senator on his return to France in 1856.

Map No: 3

Hôtel Le Tourville

★ ★ ★ ★

16 avenue de Tourville
Paris
75007

Tel: (0)1 47 05 62 62
Fax: (0)1 47 05 43 90
E-mail: hotel@tourville.com
Net: www.hoteltourville.com

Management: Michel Bouvier & Caroline Piel

On a calm tree-lined avenue, the Tourville is a comfortable, reasonably-priced 4-star hotel with an Art Deco front — but the welcome you receive is worth a skyful of stars. I enjoy talking to someone behind a fresh-flowered antique desk rather than a high counter with instant cutoff! The soft, cushioned impression in the sitting area comes from deep carpets with Turkish and Indian rugs (they lighten and colour the whole hotel), plush sofas, indoor shutters to filter the afternoon sun and muted Vivaldi. Sensuous colours and shapes abound — butter yellow, fir green, gatepost ornaments on an Empire console, soft strokable materials. We loved the ironical decorative touches, full of intelligence and fun. Each room has two or three 'finds' — a brass-handled chest of drawers, a Regency writing table, a gilt-framed mirror. And more irony in the parody paintings. The ground-floor triple is large, with its own terrace and a fascinating neo-classical group of nude women. The junior suites are also generous with space and light — and more kitschy girls in frames. Colours are peach, salmon or frankly pink; some rooms are small for the category but all have good storage space and super bathrooms (thick fluffy towels, marble finish, separate or walled-off loo), with maybe a Victorian clothes horse or an old nursery chair in contrast. To offset such simple sophistication, the vaulted breakfast room has a rustic air with its coconut matting, cane chairs and a rough patina on the pale peach-washed walls.

Rooms: 28 (4 with private terrace) & 2 junior suites with whirlpool bath.
Price: S 690-890F; D/TW 790-1090F; with terrace 1190-1390F; ST 1690-1990F.
Breakfast: With squeezed orange juice: 60F.
Meals: On request 100-300F.
Metro: Ecole Militaire; RER + Air France bus: Invalides.
Bus routes: 29 48 80 82 87 92
Car park: Ecole Militaire.

Tourville was an romantic admiral called Anne (sic) who fought pirates in the Mediterranean and spent the 1690s locked in naval battles with the English in the Channel.

Map No: 3

57

Ma Bonne dame, il est bon de brûler la chandelle aux deux bouts de temps en temps
My good woman, it's good to burn the candle at both ends from time to time.

Quelle chandelle?
What candle?

Chaillot Museums & Gardens
•
Museum of Modern Art
•
Guimet Museum
•
Radio France building

Passy – Trocadéro

Hôtel Frémiet ★★★

6 avenue Frémiet
Paris
75016

Tel: (0)1 45 24 52 06
Fax: (0)1 42 88 77 46
Net: GDS: BestWesternNo93086

Management: Madame Fourmond

 (some)

Leading off Avenue Président Kennedy, the steep little street is a glorious piece of architectural symmetry dated 1913, all in curves and juttings, stone carvings, garlands and figleaf fantasies, built as superior apartment blocks. The Frémiet has brilliantly kept the volumes and decorations of its beginnings. M Fourmond is proud to declare that although guestrooms are NOT rational here, guests are most carefully attended to. From the lovely staircase (red carpeting with brass rods and superb original windows), each landing has a grand double door into the original 10ft-high 160m² apartment, now divided up. The former drawing room, now a generous bedroom, has a curved window onto a balcony with view of the Seine, original mouldings and panelling; the master bedroom has become another excellent guestroom; the former kitchen is a huge bathroom with sensual matt-white double basins and a cockerel crowing in the tiling. Overall, it is a lesson in French apartment design just before society collapsed into the Great War. The degree of comfort quite matches the grand atmosphere. Classic Louis XV and Louis XVI pieces alongside some built-in practicalities so that all rooms have space. Recently redecorated rooms have more contemporary colour schemes and the occasional touch by the owner's designer daughter (e.g. a curved wooden bedhead or a brass rail with cushions); all are fully soundproofed. The welcome is high-class, too, and the sitting/breakfast area feels secluded and peaceful.

Rooms: 36, incl. 2 suites, with shower or bath.
Price: S 500-850F; D/TW 650-1200F; ST 1300-1800F.
Breakfast: 55F .
Meals: On request 100-200F.
Metro: Passy; RER Champ de Mars.
Bus routes: 72 32
Car park: In street or garage 200m.

In the Wine Museum just up the road, deep galleries plunge into the hillside to take you through the history of French wine. Your ticket includes a tasting; you can even lunch there.

Map No: 3

(some)

quiet big rooms

£ 68-75

Hôtel Passy-Eiffel   ★★★

10 rue de Passy
Paris
75016

Tel: (0)1 45 25 55 66
Fax: (0)1 42 88 89 88

Management: Monsieur & Madame Cantuel

When you step off the smart shopping street into the Cantuels' hotel, you can certainly believe that Passy was just a little country village a hundred years ago — you can breathe deeply in this calm atmosphere. Here, you will find a restful mix of old-fashioned and contemporary styles, where nothing is exaggerated or overdone, and a hidden patio garden with what looks like a darling little gardener's cottage across the cobbled yard, and Eiffel Tower views upstairs! There are two comfortable *salons* off the panelled hall which give onto the street through big arching windows. Indeed, there is space everywhere, by Paris standards. Rooms are decorated in firm but unaggressive colours with floral quilts and curtains. The Junior Suite I saw had four windows onto That Tower, ginger carpets and blue moiré walls, an enormously high sofabed in the sitting area, a pretty period desk, a double/twin bed with plain wooden headboard and a nice pale grey bathroom. Elsewhere you may find peach, gold and blue, or beige and deep pink; upper floors have beams and timbers; furniture is cane and wood; storage space is good — every room has a fully-mirrored cupboard — and even the smaller rooms are far from cramped. On the courtyard side, you look down onto the hotel's green patio and the next-door neighbour's very well-kept garden (he's an artist). Madame is quietly friendly and at breakfast you will learn that Monsieur is a passionate bee-keeper. You feel that they enjoy their life.

Rooms: 50, incl. 2 suites, with bath or shower.
Price: S 580-650F; D/TW 680-750F; TR 780F; ST 950-1020F.
Breakfast: 50F.
Meals: On request 80-120F.
Metro: Passy, Trocadéro; RER Boulainvilliers.
Bus routes: 22 32
Car park: 19 rue de Passy.

Less than a hundred years ago, ladies' carriages mixed with farmer's carts in the lanes of Passy and there were more churns of fresh milk carried than chic shopping bags.

Map No: 3

(some)

* * *

Hôtel Massenet
5 bis rue Massenet
Paris
75116

Tel: (0)1 45 24 43 03
Fax: (0)1 45 24 41 39
E-mail: hotel.massenet@wanadoo.fr

Management: Bernard Mathieu

For 70 years, the Mathieu family has cultivated the art of attentive welcome behind the balconied, encorbelled 1900s façade of the Massenet, and the cultivation has borne fruit: it is a most welcoming, civilised place. The ground floor, a feast of moulded panels and mirrored arches, has the atmosphere of a quiet club with deep leather armchairs, a bar and interesting pictures framed by Madame (she has a shop locally). The breakfast room, now redecorated in deep green and pale yellow, is a light fresh space that opens naturally onto the much-planted little patio where guests can sit out in summer. Upstairs, the decor is just as classically muted and relaxing: eggshell walls, dark green or deep ginger carpets with the same colour picked out again on mouldings and panels, and some bedcovers or curtains more adventurously bright. You will find one or two good pieces of old furniture, yet more interesting pictures on the walls, hanging cupboards and shelf space and room to sit peacefully. One pair of singles is suddenly much more feminine, all in satiny, musliny, peachy softness. The top floor has two rooms with terraces for intimate breakasts or aperitifs looking across miles of rooftops. Bathrooms vary, some more recently refurbished than others, one still in its 1930s originality of rounded-edge mosaics. All linen is bordered and monogrammed and all rooms except the smallest have double doors from the corridor. The feel is of deep quilted comfort and old-style class.

Rooms: 41 with bath or shower.
Price: S 505F; D/TW 685-790F.
Breakfast: 40F.
Meals: On request 70-200F.
Metro: La Muette, Passy; RER Boulainvilliers.
Bus routes: 22 32 52
Car park: 19 rue de Passy.

300 years ago, Passy was a country village where society ladies came for the fertility-enhancing waters; now it is part of metropolitan Paris where they shop and entertain.

Map No: 3

60

Hôtel Gavarni ✶ ✶

5 rue Gavarni
Paris
75116

Tel: (0)1 45 24 52 82
Fax: (0)1 40 50 16 95
E-mail: gavarni@compuserve.com
Net: www.gavarni.com

Management: Nelly Rolland

Mademoiselle Rolland! Her welcome is as warm as her laugh is silvery and you will be instantly captivated by her neat little hotel, all decked out in rich dark green and soft pale yellow. Beyond the original 1900s cast-iron and glass canopy, the atmosphere is fresh and youthful — nothing heavy or pompous here. The ground floor is mirrored and arm-chaired to a tee, the cosy breakfast area has little round tables and Bauhaus cane-and-steel tube chairs — again, a sense of unfussy airiness pervades under the mural of a pot of flowers suspended in space. Rooms, with moulded cornices, are small and neatly furnished with pale laminated units that serve their purpose well but add little charm (to be replaced in the near future). The sponged paintwork, green carpet and pastel draperies, however, are all new and repeat the basic colour scheme with various light splotchy florals for the curtains and quilted bedcovers. Showers and bathrooms are reached through space-saving folding doors; they are not big but contain all the essentials for one person at a time including good towels, while hair-dryers are mounted outside beside the full-length wall mirrors. A few rooms over the front door extend nicely into their bow windows and the 6th floor rooms seem larger despite their gently sloping ceilings. In a quiet residential side street, you are a step away from the smart shops of the Rue de Passy and a short walk from the Eiffel Tower and the Trocadéro esplanade with its museums, acrobatic roller skaters and elegant cafés.

Rooms: 30 with bath or shower.
Price: S 395F; D 500F; TW 520F.
Breakfast: 35F + à la carte.
Meals: On request 50-150F.
Metro: Passy, Trocadéro; RER Boulainvilliers.
Bus routes: 22 32
Car park: Garage Moderne, Rue de Passy.

The C19 Basque satirical cartoonist called Chevalier adopted the name *Gavarni* in memory of a geological cirque in the Pyrenees near Roland's Gap that he came to love.

Les Jardins du Trocadéro

★ ★ ★ ★

35 rue Benjamin Franklin
Paris
75116

Tel: (0)1 53 70 17 70
Fax: (0)1 53 70 17 80
E-mail: aaacademic@aol.com

Management: Katia Chekroun

Intimate, relaxed, lavish and fun — a very unusual hotel in a listed mid-C19 building. The decor is exuberantly Napoleon III, the period when gilt and orientalisms fulfilled the motto "Too much is not enough". Behind the glass front door, with its magnificent bronze leaves, two Egyptian torch-bearers salute; on landing walls, Muses beckon while Turkish-style musical monkeys gambol across door panels (all painted by Beaux Arts students). The atmosphere is young and casual — you are greeted by a delicate alabaster Beatrice aged about 14 on the front desk — but efficiency and service are there, discreet and not at all obsequious and none the worse for wear. Lovers of the small and intimate will be at home here; so will fans of French style. The gilt-mirrored, bronze-lamped *salon* has pure Second Empire furniture on a successfully aged marble floor and drinks are served at a genuine made-to-measure bistro bar, *le zinc*. Don't expect vast amounts of space in the bedrooms (the 'executive' rooms are larger and very good suites can be organised) but enjoy their soft generous draperies and the genuine period antiques (many ormolu-trimmed Boulle-type pieces) that the owners took such trouble to find; luxuriate in your whirlpool bath, surrounded by marble, then don a fluffy bathrobe before dressing for the 'worldwide tapas' served in the pretty, airy, more simply decorated basement dining room which also serves as breakfast room.

Rooms: 18 with whirlpool bath.
Price: D or TW 790-1650F; ST 1350-2600F.
Breakfast: 'Unlimited' buffet 75F.
Meals: 'La Petite Muse' restaurant: approx. 150F.
Metro: Trocadéro; RER Charles de Gaulle-Étoile.
Bus routes: 22 30 32 63
Car park: Hotel.

Franklin's active opposition to England greatly endeared him to France and the French government declared three days of national mourning when he died in 1790.

Map No: 1

Arc de Triomphe
•
Haute couture
•
Grand Palais – Petit Palais
•
Place de la Concorde
•
La Madeleine church

Étoile – Champs Élysées

(some)

Hôtel Franklin Roosevelt

* * *

18 rue Clément Marot
Paris
75008

Tel: (0)1 53 57 49 50
Fax: (0)1 47 20 44 30
E-mail: franklin@iway.fr

Management: David Le Boudec

This is, for the moment, a 'split-level' or 'sandwich' hotel and an intriguing study in change: the ground floor and two top floors have been lushly renovated by the new owners making an eminently 'English' sitting and bar area below — mahogany, red walls, leather Chesterfields, thick carpets — and high-class suites (6th floor) or big double rooms (5th floor) leading off wide, silent corridors. Up here you find air conditioning, more shiny mahogany (even the bath panels), walls cloaked in brocade or moiré and thick silky curtains hanging from big brass rods. There are subtle, sober colour schemes with 'maximum designer power' and the occasional inlaid cupboard door or whirlpool bath, stripey-marble shower or Patrick Ireland engraving to complete the sense of privilege. Plus delightful touches such as little round windows with... round curtains. Most rooms on the middle floors, called 'Japanese' or 'Bamboo' for example, have the luxury of size and are perfectly comfortable but their price reflects their greater simplicity: 'normal' size beds with white piqué covers, walls plain apart from some wonderful, ever-fresh murals (that Mississippi panorama room also has *trompe-l'œil* pictures!) and good bathrooms. But all guests naturally bathe in the plushness of the smart new communal spaces where a bright rattan-furnished breakfast room looks through to the patio, soon to be turned into a winter garden with oriental murals. Your young host is attentive and enthusiastic and you should feel well looked after.

Rooms: 47 incl. 3 suites, all with bath or shower.
Price: Standard D/TW 895-945F; renovated D/TW 1300-1800F; ST 2500-3000F.
Breakfast: Continental 65F; generous buffet 110F.
Meals: On request 100-200F.
Metro: Franklin Roosevelt; RER Charles de Gaulle-Étoile.
Bus routes: 32 42 80
Car park: George V.

At 49 rue Pierre Charron is Pershing Hall with an American Legion emblem carved over an elaborate gate and 3 window keystones depicting US sailor, soldier, airman.

Map No: 1

Hôtel de l'Élysée ★ ★ ★
12 rue des Saussaies
Paris
75008

66-76

Tel: (0)1 42 65 29 25
Fax: (0)1 42 65 64 28
Net: www.elyssaus@club-internet.fr

Management: Madame Lafond

(small)

(some)

This is a good solid value hotel, comfortable and classical but not overdoing the French style thing. Like its left-bank sister, the Ferrandi, the Elysée has *trompe-l'œil* marble panels hand-painted on the staircase walls (an art of bygone days), a real white marble fireplace and many canopied beds. Its theme is *Restauration* which, in France, refers to the early C19 post-Napoleonic, short-lived restoration of the monarchy. The basic intention is to make you feel at ease in a country-house environment with a few dramatically baroque details — a study of lamps and light fittings reveals some astounding gilded harvest sprays and spiky vegetables that might have grown in a pterodactyl's pasture. Otherwise, Jouy-pattern walls plus quilting, padding and subdued velvets are the order of the day. As usual, some 'standard' rooms are really quite small, but there is always a moulded ceiling or hand-painted cupboard. Some are fairly sombre in shades of green, brown and beige, others are covered in bright flowers. The de luxe rooms on the corner are extremely attractive with their three windows and generous space. The top-floor junior suites have great character — sloping ceilings, timbers, nooks, crannies, pretty decor. It is plush and peaceful, there's a real bar to perch at for your aperitif and marble-topped tables for breakfast. A comfort to come back to, it virtually faces the Ministry of the Interior's grand entrance on the Place Beauvau so you always have a policeman at your door.

Rooms: 32, incl. 2 suites, with bath or shower.
Price: S/D shower 660-760F; S/D bath 820-1280; TW 760-980; ST 1500F.
Breakfast: Continental plus: 65F.
Meals: Cold snacks before 8pm: 120F.
Metro: Champs Élysées, Madeleine, Miromesnil; RER Opéra-Auber.
Bus routes: 28 32 49 52 80 83 93
Car park: Hôtel Bristol.

The 'tenant' of the Place Beauvau is Interior Minister and chief of police; *saussaie* comes from *saule* = birch. In the days of birching, did the police grow their own?

Map No: 1

64

Hôtel Centre Ville Matignon
* * *

3 rue de Ponthieu
Paris
75008
Tel: (0)1 42 25 73 01
Fax: (0)1 42 56 01 39
E-mail: hcv@giga-planet.fr

Management: Alain Michaud &
Jean-François Cornillot

(late)

Paris has many imitations of the 1920s Modern Style. The Matignon is no copy, it is genuine 1924 and we love it. Enter the rectangle-upon-rectangle glazed porch, walk along the many-rectangled floor, stand under the perfect curves of the moulded ceiling light that grows out of those straight lines: you FEEL what they were saying. The lift is 1924 too, a collector's dream of iron frame and engraved glass. You will be welcomed by people who are relaxed yet sensitive to your needs, a delightful contrast to the head-office/laissez-aller atmosphere of the Champs Élysées. There's more geometric style upstairs. Each panelled door opens to reveal a large original fresco behind the bed: landscapes or near-abstract still lifes, they are very proper given the purpose for which these rooms were designed. Bathrooms have wonderfully Art Deco mod cons (basins on heavy stands with antique taps, old-fashioned tiling and trim), though some bits are definitely showing their age. Otherwise, there are discreet dark carpets, heavy curtains, coordinated quilted or textured bedcovers and head cushions (a bow to 90s fashion), black metal bedside lights (another), fine inner blinds and adequate storage. Rooms, far from enormous, have a lobby (except the junior suites where a larger lobby houses the third bed and the cupboard). An evening venue for the Parisian 'in' crowd (11pm to dawn), the scarlet and black Mathis Bar puts on virginal white cloths for your breakfast — great fun. An Airport Shuttle hotel.

Rooms: 23, incl. 5 junior suites, with bathrooms.
Price: S 590-800F; D/TW 690-900F; ST 890-1200F.
Breakfast: 55F + à la carte.
Meals: On request 100-150F.
Metro: Champs Élysées-Clémenceau; RER Charles de Gaulle-Étoile.
Bus routes: 28 32 42 49 73 93
Car park: Champs Élysées.

Mansions were built here in the 1700s (the Élysée Palace, for example, for La Pompadour); in the 1800s, the 'Élysian Fields' were covered with modest houses; in the 1920s activity was less modest...

Map No: 1

Hôtel des Champs-Élysées   **

2 rue d'Artois
Paris
75008

Tel: (0)1 43 59 11 42
Fax: (0)1 45 61 00 61

Management: Madame Monteil

Nothing is too much for Madame Monteil. She will even provide a little talc to ease swollen feet into tight boots during a heatwave. The art of hospitality has been handed down from her grandparents, first in the family to own the hotel; their delightful pre-war pictures adorn one wall. The unpretentious façade on a little street behind the Champs Élysées speaks for the simple, gracious reception you will receive inside. There are deep leather sofas in the 1930s-style lobby and a welcoming bar beneath an Art Deco mural of a *trompe-l'œil* theatre curtain. There is elegance in the staircase with its blue and grey decor. Since this 'back' street may carry occasional posses of departing clubbers, bedrooms (all but six give onto the street) are fully soundproofed and air-conditioned; each has a custom-made stained-wood bedhead and framed desktop unit neatly incorporating the minibar. Covers and curtains are often made of English fabrics, subtly coordinated with pastel-pink, cream-sponged or turquoise walls for lighter or darker effect; wall-mounted bedside lights are cleancut and well-placed and mirrored cupboards provide adequate storage. Bathrooms are small but just as recently renovated in smart grey, silver, black and white tiles or beige marble and some ingenious quarter-circle shower stalls. With fresh baker's croissants and bread for breakfast, we thought we had found remarkable value in an expensive neighbourhood — and exceptional human contact.

Rooms: 31 with shower; 4 with bath.
Price: D (shower) 475F; TW (bath) 560F; extra bed 80F.
Breakfast: 44F.
Meals: No.
Metro: St Philippe du Roule, Franklin Roosevelt; RER Charles de Gaulle-Étoile.
Bus routes: 22 28 32 73 80 83 93
Car park: Rue de Ponthieu.

Amazingly, in the present-day artificiality of the area, this street was the Royal (and Revolutionary, and Imperial) plants nursery from 1640 to 1826.

Map No: 1

Induire quelqu'un en erreur
Lead someone astray

Après ça, il nous faudrait juste une petite chambre pour deux Rive Gauche.
After that, all we need is a little room for two on the Left Bank

Parc Monceau gardens

•

St Ferdinand

•

Bois de Boulogne

•

Jardin d'Acclimatation

Étoile – Porte Maillot

Hôtel Kléber   ***
7 rue de Belloy   **Tel:** (0)1 47 23 80 22
Paris   **Fax:** (0)1 49 52 07 20
75116   **E-mail:** kleberhot@aol.com

Management: Samuel Abergel

Those ornate double-framed gilt mirrors come from a derelict château that was auctioned off piece by piece — the Chekrouns, who also own the Académie and the Jardins du Trocadéro, love hunting for such things to furnish their hotels. Behind the mid-C19 façade with its wonderful wrought-iron balconies, the atmosphere at the Kléber is determinedly traditional French *romantique*; witness the gilt-bronze-encrusted curly chests, elaborate lamps (one of the large twin rooms has an astounding 'desk' light with hefty bronze stems and three big bunches of electrified (sic) grapes), period paintings and oriental touches such as lifesize statues. The suite has a beautiful roll-top desk with Chinese inlay in its generous balconied *salon* (which clients often use as a meeting room), unusual 5-drawer bedside tables in its king-size bedded bedroom, and even a kitchenette. All the decor is rich in colour — reds, yellows, blues — and texture in the smaller rooms too, all bedding is new and the six twin beds can be zipped together into king-size doubles; bathrooms are finished with tiles or mosaic and have all the necessary bits including power showers. Samy's warm welcome is confirmed by the basket of fruit and chocolates awaiting you in your room. In the newly-refurbished ground-floor area, the breakfast buffet includes homemade jams and croissants as well as cereals, cheese and eggs for a fine start to the day. English, Spanish, Hebrew, Japanese and Arabic spoken!

Rooms: 22 with bath or shower, including 1 suite.
Price: S/D or TW 960-1290F; ST 1590F.
Breakfast: Full buffet 60F.
Meals: On request 100-150F.
Metro: Kléber; RER Charles de Gaulle-Étoile.
Bus routes: 22 30
Car park: Hotel.

Kléber, soldier son of an Alsatian pastry cook, couldn't, as a commoner, hope for officer rank in the King's army but rose fast after the Revolution and died a General under Napoleon.

Hôtel Résidence Foch

* * *

10 rue Marbeau
Paris
75116

Tel: (0)1 45 00 46 50
Fax: (0)1 45 01 98 68

Management: Patrick Schneider

Beautiful People parade these streets! From the original iron-framed glass door of the hotel, in its blessedly quiet side street, you can see the trees of what is still the smartest address in Paris — Avenue Foch. You enter a cosy, traditional, cushioned French hotel interior that is reassuring rather than striking, comfortable rather than designed. The unhotelly pink towels and sheets are an indication of the solid family atmosphere the Schneiders convey: they have been here — father, mother and son — for a long time. The perfectly French decor seeks not to excite but to relax yet dares to use deep orangey red cloth for some walls, rich blue carpets in apartments and little gilt-painted chairs in the 'Gold Room' (which really has gold-sheen walls, a very unusual antique gilded chest of drawers and yellow-streaked curtains) as well as pink and blue paisleys and gently oriental leafy patterns. The top two floors have antiques such as a Napoleonic 'Egyptian Campaign' chest of drawers, an old school desk or one of those lovely old country *armoires*. The lower floors are furnished with more modern custom-made Louis XVI-style pieces that have been properly streak-painted in the right shades of pastel. Bathrooms, tiled with the occasional decorative motif, have liquid soap dispensers, paper tissues and glass tooth mugs. The breakfast room is lit by a small green courtyard, the sitting area is rich yet restful and the family welcomes you with natural hospitality.

Rooms: 25, incl. 4 suites, with bathrooms.
Price: S 620-670F; D/TW 670-800F; ST 880-910F.
Breakfast: Buffet 55F.
Meals: No.
Metro: Argentine, Porte Maillot; RER Charles de Gaulle-Étoile, Porte Maillot.
Bus routes: PC (Marbeau stop), Air France bus.
Car park: Foch or Palais des Congrès.

J-B Marbeau (1798-1875), horrified by the lot of young children of working mothers, founded the first *crèche* in 1844 and spread the idea throughout Europe.

Map No: 1

Hôtel Résidence Impériale
★ ★ ★

155 avenue Malakoff
Paris
75116
Tel: (0)1 45 00 23 45
Fax: (0)1 45 01 88 82
E-mail: res.imperiale@wanadoo.fr
Net: www.paris-charming-hotels.com

Management: Pierre Salles

In spite of the grand name this is far from being a snooty hostelry. Indeed, behind the masses of geraniums that dangle down the façade, the young owner and his staff are enthusiastic, energetic, humorous and relaxed. Given the very closeness of its huge neighbour, Paris's international conference centre (in the process of being virtually doubled in size, to boot), it is inevitably much prized by business and conference people, but it is friendly and comfortable for all that. Pierre Salles has renovated his old hotel from top to bottom, installed double glazing, double windows and air conditioning — essential for rooms over the busy avenue — and chosen simple, made-to-measure furniture units in natural wood to make the best use of the space in each room. We particularly enjoyed the original lamps, like leather-covered urns, giving off a softening light. The bedding is firm, the upholstery richly quilted, the curtains thick and generous, the wallpaper unobtrusive. Top-floor rooms have exposed timbers and sloping ceilings for a bit of character; those at the back look out over a row of small private gardens and a rather lovely old curved redbrick building. And when you go back down to street level, the smart redecorated sitting area is laid out in several little open *salons* for privacy and you can have the pleasure of the small patio for breakfast or evening drinks. If you are cooped up all day in the Palais des Congrès or arrive by airport bus at the Porte Maillot, this is a nearby haven.

Rooms: 37 with bathrooms.
Price: S 690-790F; D/T 740-840F; TR 890-1010F.
Breakfast: 55F with a large choice.
Meals: On request 80 -150F.
Metro + RER + Air France bus: Porte Maillot.
Bus routes: 73 82 PC
Car park: Palais des Congrès.

Malakoff was a bastion at Sebastopol that fell to Marshal MacMahon in the Crimean War after he (not Julius Caesar) had declared famously *"J'y suis, j'y reste"*.

Map No: 1

Hôtel Pergolèse

* * * *

3 rue Pergolèse
Paris
75116

Tel: (0)1 53 64 04 04
Fax: (0)1 53 64 04 40
E-mail: pergolese@wanadoo.fr

Management: Madame Édith Vidalenc

So near the Arc de Triomphe, pass the intriguing sliding doors and leave C19 Paris behind you: here is a refreshing festival of contemporary design where room shapes, use of light and materials, purpose-designed furniture and minute details of glassware all add up. Édith Vidalenc works closely with sought-after designer Rena Dumas to keep a sleek but warmly colourful, curvaceously human hotel. Her own sense of hospitality conditions staff attitudes: the faithful team at reception know all the regulars and are leagues away from the frostiness that so often passes for 'de luxe' treatment. Hilton McConnico did the pictures and the brilliant carpet in the new bar. Materials are wood, leather and polished metal. The leitmotiv shape is the arch over the main doorway, repeated in leaf-like ash bedheads, lobby sofas before curved glass walls onto the patio, table legs and chrome 'tureen' washbasins. The general pastel tones are mutedly smart so the dark-coloured breakfast room gives a slightly humorous wake-up nudge. Indeed, not taking oneself too seriously while doing a really professional job is the keynote here. Rooms, fairly small except for the top-floor *Pergolèse*, are all similarly furnished in pale wood and leather with thick unpatterned curtains and white bedcovers in a soft skin-like material. The star *Pergolèse* room, lit by sloping rooflights, is a small masterpiece in palest apricot with a few spots of bright colour and a superb open bathroom.

Rooms: 40 with bathrooms.
Price: S 1000-1300F; D or TW 1100-1500F; Pergolèse 1800F for two.
Breakfast: 70F in room; 90F buffet.
Meals: Very light meals c.150F.
Metro: Argentine; RER + Air France bus Porte Maillot.
Bus routes: 73 82
Car park: Place Saint Ferdinand.

The Porte Maillot's expanding conference centre and motor traffic were not ever thus: from 1830 to 1930 it was a huge, much-frequented fun fair, the "Luna Park".

Hôtel Centre Ville Étoile ***

6 rue des Acacias
Paris
75017

Tel: (0)1 43 80 56 18
Fax: (0)1 47 54 93 43
E-mail: hcv@giga-planet.fr

Management: Alain Michaud

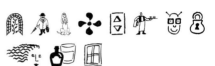

This tiny hotel has a very definite style; for once, tiny has not meant cosy. I like it for its difference. The shiny black reception desk — and the 20-foot ficus tree — are in a 3-storey galleried well of light that gives onto a quiet, plant-filled cul-de-sac. I was very taken with the ingenuity and originality of the space. The view from the top gallery is an engineer's delight, across metal frame and curtain wall. The decor may be a little sombre for some; it is based on an Art Deco style that dictates the black and white colour scheme, with a chromatic glance at American Surrealism in the shape of a large original 1930s oil and two very big 'romantic' country scenes on gallery landings. There are prints from American cartoon strips and black carpeting with slippy grey-white stripes like running water everywhere. Rooms are small but spaces are well used, though storage remains limited. They can be masculine (pale brown wall covering, brown and black abstract bedheads, covers and curtains, one black and one red chair), or more pastel-shaded (blue covers with 1950s-style coloured-print curtains), or elegant white, cream and grey mixtures. Bathrooms have white fittings, round basins, restful grey tiling, lots of mirrors and bathrobes. In contrast, bright red oriental-print cloths (on black tables) and airy Bauhaus wire chairs enliven the basement breakfast room. With so few rooms, staff have plenty of time to be friendly, helpful and really welcoming. The Airport Shuttle operates here.

Rooms: 15 with bathrooms.
Price: S 590-790F; D 690-890F;
TW 690-950F.
Breakfast: 55F.
Meals: On request 100-150F.
Metro: Argentine; RER & Air France
bus: Charles de Gaulle-Étoile.
Bus routes: 43 73 92 93
Car park: 24 rue des Acacias.

In 1834, Louis Philippe's heir apparent took a fast bend nearby, fell out of his carriage and was killed. Banal? Yes, but few crash victims have Byzantine chapels built in their memory (St Ferdinand).

Map No: 1

71

Hôtel Étoile Saint-Ferdinand ★★★

36 rue Saint Ferdinand
Paris
75017

Tel: (0)1 45 72 66 66
Fax: (0)1 45 74 12 92
E-mail: ferdinan@paris-honotel.com/honore@paris-honotel.com
Net: www.paris-honotel.com

Management: Agnès Bourdon

The frontage looks as if the original dressed stone wall was sliced up into 'columns' and the lobby is quite surprising too, with those ancient pitted timbers joining a very modern mirrored reception desk to an equally modern spotlit ceiling. But otherwise there is nothing eccentric about this peaceful, solidly comfortable Right-Bank hotel run by a quiet manageress and her cheerful staff. In the two airy *salon* areas you sit on cream-caned green-cushioned Louis XVI; to reach the breakfast room you go past a couple more Louis XVI corners then find ochre walls, white dado, yellow tablecloths and black cane chairs under a frosted skylight (it was nice to see a baby's high chair too) — a light and pleasant atmosphere in which to enjoy your freshly-squeezed juice. All bedrooms give onto a courtyard or one of two quiet streets; the six courtyard rooms for three are larger than the others and have space for a low table and extra chairs. Here, the decor is a subtle wallpaper in pale apricot with a fine eggshell-white pattern in harmony with the patina-painted Louis XVI elements that are found throughout. Bedcovers are made of richly thick white piqué and curtains are just nets and white blackouts (!). The overall effect is one of simplicity; each room has mirrored sliding cupboard doors, a minibar incorporated in the desk unit and an Impressionist print. Unexciting, but reliable value near the great conference centre at Porte Maillot and a short walk from the Arc de Triomphe.

Rooms: 42 with bathrooms.
Price: S/D/TW 750-1000F; child under 12 free in parents' room.
Breakfast: Continental plus: 60F.
Meals: On request 90-150F.
Metro: Argentine, Porte Maillot; RER: Charles de Gaulle-Étoile, Porte Maillot.
Bus routes: 43 73 PC Air France bus
Car park: Rue Brunel.

The strangely unfinished-looking monument to Léon Serpollet on the square might be a homage to a protector of the poor. He actually invented the steam-driven tricycle.

Map No: 1

72

Hôtel Flaubert

**

19 rue Rennequin
Paris
75017

Tel: (0)1 46 22 44 35
Fax: (0)1 43 80 32 34

Management: Michel & Christiane
Niceron

On a quiet little street just "ten slow minutes' walk" from the Arc de Triomphe, you will be received by an easy, kindly couple who are generous with one of of their most valuable possessions — their time. They also share their passion for felines (who only live here in the form of graven images). The Flaubert's other surpassing asset is its miniature jungle, a long narrow courtyard between two parts of the building connected by wooden stairs and bridges where a riot of flowering plants and greenery flourishes. This could be the depths of Normandy, the great Gustave Flaubert's home county, or even some tropical haven, and it is most un-Parisian to walk through the bushes and up the outside stairs to your room under the eaves (or you can take the lift, of course). The breakfast room, with its big windows onto the street and yet more green life, has bent-wood chairs, floral cushions and Provençal floor tiles to prolong the country feel. The overall decor is very simple with little variation. All doors and paintwork, for example, are pink; carpets are brown or dark red, bedroom furniture is Italian rattan — light and not at all overbearing, but there is always a table and one or two chairs or a stool. Much attention has been paid to details like table lamps and the soft pastels and quilts used throughout are supremely restful. Bathrooms are good and the larger rooms have plenty of storage. Altogether excellent value. And they are such a delightful couple.

Rooms: 37 with bath or shower.
Price: S 390-480F; D/TW 480-550F;
TR 700F.
Breakfast: Continental plus: 40F.
Meals: No.
Metro: Ternes, Pereire; RER Pereire,
Charles de Gaulle-Étoile.
Bus routes: 30 31 43 84 92 93
Car park: Fiat opposite hotel.

In 1682, Rennequin built the magnificent *Machine de Marly* which, for 120 years, propelled water up to the great fountains at Versailles using 14 wheels and 221 pumps.

Map No: 1

Hôtel Eber ★★★

18 rue Léon Jost
Paris
75017

Tel: (0)1 46 22 60 70
Fax: (0)1 47 63 01 01
Net: www.planetpsyche.com/eber.htm

Management: Jean-Marc Eber

Jean-Marc Eber instantly communicates his enthusiasm and his pleasure in welcoming guests to his small, charming hotel. We like the lighthearted approach married to very professional management. Also, the wonderfully quiet Eber is a *Relais Silence* hotel. You may meet top models, fashion designers or other film folk appropriate to this smart neighbourhood where 'de luxe' groceries and chocolates can also be found. The documents that decorate the walls will lead you through the building of the Statue of Liberty in a nearby yard. And you can borrow a house umbrella in your hour of need — a superior touch, perhaps inspired by the two umbrella-toting slave boys sitting on the mantelpiece? The intimate salon and bar/breakfast area are good places to sit and tuck into breakfast, served at any hour with 15 sorts of jam and 3 teas. Rooms vary in size, some are quite small, some have grandly high ceilings; the duplexes are large enough for families and the one with private terrace is particularly seductive. Fairly neutral colour schemes with pastel print curtains and covers, strengthened by the occasional dark medieval-type stripe, make them all very restful. Nice old gilt-framed mirrors, the odd carved *armoire*, bring a touch of the antique; storage space is generally adequate. Bathrooms are pleasingly tiled and fitted and we like the 'olde' look of the cast-iron towel rails on wooden brackets. A delightful yet professional host, too.

Rooms: 18, incl. 2 duplex, with bath or shower.
Price: S/D 660-710F; duplex 1150F or 1460F.
Breakfast: 55F.
Meals: On request c. 160F.
Metro: Courcelles; RER Charles de Gaulle-Étoile, Pereire.
Bus routes: 30 84
Car park: 200m Elf garage.

Nearby, do visit the two little-known, superbly furnished mansion-museums, treasure houses of French design and taste: Nissim de Camondo and Jacquemart André.

Map No: 1

74

Hôtel Médéric   **

4 rue Médéric   **Tel:** (0)1 47 63 69 13
Paris   **Fax:** (0)1 44 40 05 33
75017

Management: Bernard Rolin

In a residential area just a step away from smart Parc Monceau, near the Champs Élysées, the Médéric is run by a brother and sister who inherited the gift of hospitality from their hotelier parents. Madame is the most elegant, friendly, Parisienne grandmother you could imagine. She believes you should come to an hotel as you go to the theatre: for something you wouldn't find at home. So, making the most of the small rooms and banal built-in units they found when they arrived, the Rolins have put gilt-bronze light fittings over the beds (spiky flower sprays or swirly-stemmed, white-petalled, Catherine wheels that make you laugh outright with delight), a fine old mirror in each room, a very French padded armchair wherever there is space. Rooms are mostly small, bathrooms adequate, shower rooms tiny, but the two long top-floor rooms are larger with their sloping ceilings and roof windows, skirted tables and French chairs, and can take three or four people. Lit by a baroque torch-bearing servant boy, the ground-floor breakfast/sitting area is most attractive. With a deep grey plush sofa, a couple of moss-green armchairs and a red-skirted table, it feels like a French family *salon*; the grey and yellow dining room is charming and through a glass wall a mirror reflects it all back, doubling the depth. A friendly, intimate, good-value two-star with "the best beds in Paris" (said a regular guest I met there).

Rooms: 27 with bath or shower.
Price: S 425F; D 425-495F; TW 575-620F; TR/Q 750F.
Breakfast: 45F.
Meals: No.
Metro: Courcelles; RER Charles de Gaulle-Étoile.
Bus routes: 30 84
Car park: Rue de Courcelles.

Nearby Avenue de Wagram is named for an Austrian village where Napoleon won a 'resounding victory' over the Archduke — 20 000 dead versus 22 000. Howzat!

Map No: 1

Hôtel Cheverny   ***
7 villa Berthier
Paris
75017

Tel: (0)1 42 12 44 00
Fax: (0)1 47 63 26 62

Management: Monsieur Brillant & Monsieur Gillot

The Cheverny's character comes from unexpected vistas and twists in its layout. With two buildings and the gaps between them, the owners have created a series of tiny hanging gardens and patios overlooked by glazed landings transformed into tempting little sitting areas; there are plants everywhere, flowers of all colours in summer. The style is cleanly modern with 1930s touches. Colours are pale and restful, dove-grey with dark blue, deep biscuit with pale cream and 'ethnic' woven patchwork for a touch of fresh brightness. The bedroom units are elegant and unobtrusive with disguised minibars, mirror-fronted cupboards, suitcase spaces beneath (an intelligent detail) and firm beds. Bathrooms are just as coolly attractive with a neat clothes-line (another good mark). The new junior suites are stunningly, warmly chic — deep grey and bright gold stripes on thick dark blue carpet with two smart red French armchairs, for example. Other rooms are smaller, reflected in the price, all have good storage and the latest telephone/ansaphone systems plus modem socket. In summer, you can breakfast in the leafy patio, otherwise in the light and generous basement breakfast area (generous buffet too). Just a stone's throw from the lively boulevard, 5 minutes' walk from the Porte Maillot conference centre, 15 from the Arc de Triomphe — here is a place to sleep peacefully in stylish surroundings. They also have a fine seminar room and use of the Airport Shuttle service.

Rooms: 48 with bath or shower.
Price: S 540-610F; D 610-690F; TW 650-810F TR 910F; ST 810F.
Breakfast: Buffet 60F.
Meals: On request 90-150F.
Metro: Porte Champerret; RER Pereire.
Bus routes: 84 92 93 PC
Car park: Porte Champerret.

In 1874, in the heyday of steam, the Boulevard Berthier was chosen to test a new single-rail steam-tram. It scared its testers and was not put into production.

Map No: 1

Hôtel de Banville
166 boulevard Berthier
Paris
75017

***

Tel: (0)1 42 67 70 16
Fax: (0)1 44 40 42 77
E-mail: hotelbanville@wanadoo.fr
Net: www.hotelbanville.fr

Management: Marianne Moreau-Lambert

So deliciously Parisian an hotel: smart, with fine period furniture and the elegance of inherited style, yet soft and welcoming like a private home. The Lambert family, who have owned it for generations, love their *métier* and are proud of being their own, very competent, interior designers. They also make their own light meals, including the homemade *pâté auvergnat*. The reception/sitting area is large and gracious with its bar, deep sofas and piano under the tolerant eye of elaborately framed Old Masters, mirrors and clocks. The bedrooms are full of light, pale colours and intimacy. The two new top-floor rooms are magnificent: 'Marie's' open apartment is superbly subtle in tones of natural stone and earth, from palest eggshell to rich red loam, with a gauzily romantic white-canopied bed, a real, sloping-ceilinged sitting room giving onto a delicious little terrace (breakfast here with the Eiffel Tower) and a brilliant bathroom in the middle with thick double curtains for soft partitioning; 'Amélie', sunnily feminine in pale yellow and soft ginger, rejoices in her own balcony and a fine new, but old-style, bathroom (separate wc's in both). The other rooms are equally delightful with their gentle, airy, soft-quilt-on-firm-mattress touch, period and modern furniture and excellent bathrooms. Staff — many have worked here for years — are as friendly as the owners and the motto of the house might be 'Meet the client's expectation before it is put into words'. Excellent public transport to all parts of Paris.

Rooms: 38 with bathrooms.
Price: S 760F; D 890F; 'Amélie'
1050F; ST 'Marie' 1450F.
Breakfast: 65F.
Meals: Light meals 50F to 150F.
Metro: Porte de Champerret, Pereire;
RER Pereire.
Bus routes: 92 84 93 PC
Car Park: Rue de Courcelles.

Covered with titles and glory by Napoleon, Berthier died defenestrated, either due to a fit of insanity or the actions of 6 masked men "seen in the vicinity at that time". We shall never know.

Map No: 1

Hôtel de Neuville ★★★

3 rue Verniquet
Paris
75017

Tel: (0)1 43 80 26 30
Fax: (0)1 43 80 38 55
E-mail: neuville@hotellerie.net

£75
Good
Breakfast

Management: Madame Beherec &
Karine Gachet

Its white stone façade with geranium-filled windowboxes overlooks a quiet square just off the Boulevard Pereire. You will be welcomed by a young and enthusiastic staff in the large, airy, split-level lobby where light floods in through the arched windows. It feels like a club with its oak-tinted armchairs, low tables, bar stools and interesting works by contemporary painters. Your eye is then drawn past two pairs of Ionic columns towards the little patio, all greenery and pots and lovely stones giving a sense of space and peace. And the basement breakfast room has a wonderful surprise: the patio is down here too, the green light and air skillfully augmented with mirrors. This is definitely a family-run hotel. Madame manages it with Monsieur (they also own the left-bank Clos Médicis), designs and makes the draperies, supervises her children's homework when they are out of school and is still a charming, relaxed hostess. There are two 'honeymoon' rooms sporting canopied beds with voluptuous blowsy curtains. The rooms over the boulevard are a good size, well-lit and the higher you are the more you can see of the Sacré Coeur. Colours are soft orange with salmon pink in bold chintzes, paisleys or gentle florals; the furniture is comfortable with some brass bedsteads, some plain pine; there is decent storage space, the occasional antique mirror, old lamps and prints from Old Masters to remind us of the building's C19 origins. A quiet, friendly place to stay. I found the atmosphere most relaxing.

Rooms: 28 with bathrooms.
Price: S/D 750F. Extra person 150F.
Breakfast: 55F with cheese, yoghurt, hard-boiled eggs, fresh fruit, cereals.
Meals: Light lunches 100-120F on weekdays.
Metro & RER: Pereire.
Bus routes: 84 92 93
Car park: Hotel or Boulevard Berthier.

The environment was improved 3 years ago when a nursery school and tennis courts were built over the metro. Add the trees and you have the complete village atmosphere.

Map No: 1

(78)

Le Service

St Augustin
•
Grévin waxworks museum
•
Department stores
•
Stock Exchange (Bourse)

Opera – Grands Boulevards

Hôtel Newton Opéra ★ ★ ★

11bis rue de l'Arcade
Paris
75008

Tel: (0)1 42 65 32 13
Fax: (0)1 42 65 30 90
Net: www.integra.fr/newtonopera

Management: Monsieur Simian & Madame Tobrouki

The little attentions count so much! You will find a pretty flask of mandarine liqueur and two tiny goblets beside the dish of *pot pourri* in your room, a superbly finished bathroom (I especially liked the grey pinstripe tiling) with cotton buds, makeup remover pads, a gilded soap dish, a magnifying mirror... Off a quiet side street, only a few hundred yards from Paris's renowned and thronging department stores, enter under the red awnings and let the Newton Opéra enfold you in soft, peaceful elegance. The big ground-floor *salon* is peach plush and has period pieces on oriental rugs, a good place to read the day's papers. The breakfast room is a classic stone vault with high-backed chairs and a generous buffet, the prints and engravings all remind you of the artistic heyday of the turn of the (last) century. Bedrooms are not large but they are eminently attractive in their colourful dress: be they yellow and green or pink and green or all blue, the furniture is appropriately old-painted Louis XVI or polished rustic with a delicate chair or two, a long gilt-framed mirror... and a modem socket. There are two special rooms on the sixth floor — each has a private, shrubbed and flowered balcony with breakfast table for two and a lounger; book early, they are much coveted. Or try the bargain weekend offer with room, champagne and a night out in the price. As a long-standing Egyptian client told me: "The room is deliciously cosy, the bathroom has everything you need and they are so friendly here".

Rooms: 31, incl. 1 triple, with bath or shower.
Price: S/D 750F (shower) & 850F (bath); TR 930F.
Breakfast: Buffet 60F.
Meals: On request approx. 160F.
Metro: Madeleine, Havre-Caumartin; RER Auber.
Bus routes: 22 27 42 52 53 66 Roissybus
Car park: Rue Chauveau Lagarde.

La Madeleine took time to find its religious feet: started in 1764, stopped during the Revolution, named Temple of Fame by Napoleon, it was finally consecrated in 1842.

Map No: 1

Hôtel Chopin ✶✶

10 boulevard Montmartre
(46 passage Jouffroy)
Paris
75009

Tel: (0)1 47 70 58 10
Fax: (0)1 42 47 00 70

Management: Philippe Bidal

Behind that delightful 1850s frontage across the end of this typical Parisian shopping arcade, the light airy lobby has always been upstaged by its green china pot, beautifully copied in France when Chinoiserie was all the rage. Smiles are freely given, people are pleased to see you, but pianists beware — the piano hasn't been tuned for years. All rooms give onto courtyards (so no noise) and low rooftops, the most stunning being the zinc expanses covering the Grévin waxworks museum (sleep deeply above bloody scenes of French Revolution). I was dazzled by the roofer's craft here : the *Salle des Papillons* looks like a medieval apsed chapel, the glass roof of the arcade like a vast upturned hull. The rooms are mostly a good size for the price; bathrooms are modern, simple and functional — one has an atticky 'sulking' corner with chair. Stairs and corridors, now redecorated, are extremely elegant with rich green carpet, grasspaper walls, nicely-framed prints lit by 'Old Master' lights and some fine table lamps. The recently renovated rooms have vibrant, modern colour schemes (deep salmon, bright yellow or raspberry walls, rich green carpets and matching upholstery). Furniture is plain and simple; there are some pretty white chairs with hand-applied transfer motifs and a clever cane table with two chairs 'nesting' underneath it. The bedding is good firm foam. Monsieur Bidal's grandmother's water colours add class to the welcoming breakfast room of this supremely pleasant and friendly hotel.

Rooms: 36 bath or shower (one with separate wc).
Price: S 405-435F; D 450-490F; TR 565F.
Breakfast: Buffet 38F.
Meals: No.
Metro: Richelieu-Drouot; RER Opéra-Auber.
Bus routes: 49 67 74 85
Car park: Rue Chauchat.

The moose's head over No 34 is made of papier maché: M Segas used to work in the theatre. He now sells a fascinating variety of antique canes... and some genuine glass eyes.

Ils ne savent où donner de la tête
They don't know which way to turn

Elle a fondu dans ses bras
She melted in his arms

Montmartre

Hôtel Le Bouquet de Montmartre ★★

1 rue Durantin
Paris
75018

Tel: (0)1 46 06 87 54
Fax: (0)1 46 06 09 09
Net: www.bouquetdemontmartre.com

Management: Jennifer Gibergues

The Bouquet de Montmartre has had a much-needed facelift and the great spread of repainted outside wall is now in keeping with the inside which still lives up to its name (origin unknown) — sweet, flowery and boudoir-like. A good 2-star hotel, it may not be to everyone's taste but it is all-of-a-piece, a lesson in a particular type of French interior. The black and white mosaic floor is eye-boggling; the decor is all flock 'brocade' wallpaper, glue-on mouldings and curlicues, curvy sideboards and Louis XVI chairs. The breakfast room is lit by large windows onto the square... and vast numbers of mottled-glass light fittings on walls and ceilings. This careful decoration covers the stairs and landings, with lights set in niches and moulded ceiling wells. The original 1920s banisters are painted white and gold to match and all doors are 'leather'-padded. The rooms vary — some are still being renovated — but the design principle is beds in alcoves with myriad little cupboards around, plus hanging space, and candle-shaped lights. Curtains and bedcovers are generally the same material — red and green striped satiny stuff or muted blue and beige velvet or textured ethnic print — and the newer bath/shower rooms treated in two-coloured mosaic tiling. Mattresses are firm foam and recent. The Gibergues family work hard at keeping up with their large household and still have time to sit and chat with their guests. Friendly, simple, in one of the prettiest squares in Paris and excellent value.

Rooms: 36 with bath or shower.
Price: S/D 360-420F; TR 465F.
Breakfast: 30F.
Meals: No.
Metro: Abbesses; RER Gare du Nord.
Bus routes: 30 54 67 68 74 80 95
Car park: Place Clichy.

You emerge from the metro at Abbesses under one of the finest remaining Art Nouveau canopies by Hector Guimard deliciously blending into its leafy surroundings.

Map No: 2

Hôtel Caulaincourt   *

2 square Caulaincourt
63/65 rue Caulaincourt
Paris
75018

Tel: (0)1 46 06 42 99
Fax: (0)1 46 06 48 67

Management: Monsieur Hacène

Paris-by-the-Seine can be sweltering and unbreathable; come up to the top, to Montmartre, and perch on the airy hillside. The Caulaincourt gives onto two steep slopes — one of those vertiginous staircases on one side and a scruffy, wildly woody slope of a communal space at the back. It is a basic place to stay — at these prices, what else would you expect? — in an exquisitely privileged position. The 'mountain air' sweeps through the warren-like corridors and the rooms are simple and spotless. The garden is virtually unusable but a blessed source of fresh air and quiet (except when the teenagers in the next-door building blast a momentary techno-rave over their mammoth decibel machines, but this is short-lived); there is some double glazing but no real need for it. This is the peaceful and bourgeois part of Montmartre yet you can walk up to Place du Tertre and the Sacré Coeur in 5 minutes. The lobby and breakfast room, directly off the leafy impasse (with its excellent café-restaurant) are as straightforward as the rest. Rooms are plainly furnished with decent firm bedding, candlewick bedcovers, very adequate bedside lights and shower rooms (where applicable — more are installed each year), and harmless wallpapers. All the decoration is reviewed once a year and refreshed where necessary. No frills, but excellent value and good basic service (radical plans suggest a lift and full shower rooms for the front 16 rooms — let us know!).

Rooms: 50 with basin, shower or shower & wc.
Price: S basin 145F; D basin 180F; D shower 230F; D shower wc 280F; TR shower 280F; TR shower wc 310.
Breakfast: 25F.
Meals: No.
Metro: Lamarck-Caulaincourt; RER Gare du Nord.
Bus routes: 80
Car park: Place Clichy.

Having renounced his peerage, Caulaincourt was a foot soldier during the Revolution, an ardent follower of Napoleon, a friend of Tsar Alexander, and still managed to die in his bed.

Map No: 2

Useful Vocabulary

**Some useful words and expressions
to help you avoid ending up like this** ·········▶

**Paumé
Dropout; lost case**

Bolster	*Un Traversin*
Blanket	*Une Couverture*
Towel	*Une Serviette*
Tea; herb tea	*Un Thé; Une Infusion*
Ice	*De la glace*
Ice-cream; Mirror	*Une glace*
Glass	*Un Verre*
Coat hangers	*Des Cintres*
Light bulb; Blister	*Une Ampoule*
Sticking plaster	*Du Sparadrap (sic)*
Soap; Shampoo	*Du Savon; Du Shampooing*
Lavatory paper	*Du Papier toilette*
Fan	*Un Ventilateur*
Out of order/broken	*En panne/cassé*
Stuck	*Coincé*
The room is too small/big/ noisy/quiet/expensive/cheap	*La chambre est trop petite/grande/ bruyante/tranquille/chère/bon marché.*
May I please have a pillow.	*Je voudrais un oreiller, s'il vous plaît.*
May I leave my children/wife/ husband with the concierge?	*Pourrais-je laisser mes enfants/ma femme/ mon mari avec le concierge?*
I can't open the window.	*Je n'arrive pas à ouvrir la fenêtre.*
Where can I find some fresh air?	*Où peut-on trouver un peu d'air?*
May I have a room over the garden/courtyard?	*Je voudrais une chambre sur le jardin/la cour.*
Get out of my room!	*Sortez de ma chambre!*
Leave me alone!	*Laissez-moi tranquille!*
Is this really tea?	*C'est vraiment du thé ça?*
The shower/bath/loo is blocked.	*La douche/la baignoire/le wc est bouché.*
My wallet/key/baby is locked in the cupboard.	*J'ai enfermé mon porte-monnaie/ma clé/mon bébé dans l'armoire.*
How old is this bread?	*De quand date ce pain?*
My bed sags/is hard/soft.	*Mon lit est défoncé/trop dur/trop mou.*
The cold water is hot.	*L'eau froide est chaude.*
I've scalded the baby.	*J'ai échaudé le bébé.*
Call a doctor please.	*Appelez un médecin s'il vous plaît.*
There is no plug for the basin/ bath.	*Il n'y a pas de bouchon pour lelavabo/ la baignoire.*
Please remove that spider.	*Enlevez cette araignée, s'il vous plaît.*

Je vais faire la grasse matinée.	I'm going to have a lie in.
J'en ai ras le bol.	I'm fed up (with this).
J'en ai marre.	I'm sick of this.
C'est marrant ça.	That's funny (peculiar or ha!ha!).
Se marrer.	To laugh.
Oh la vache!	What a cow!/Oh lord!/How awful!
C'est vachement bien ça.	That's really great.

To enliven your reading of the entries in this book and perhaps illumine your stay in the hotels listed, here is a very brief history of French furniture in the 17th, 18th and 19th centuries with the essential features of each style, an illustration by Mathias Fournier and the dates of the king or government associated with the name (the period often covers more time than the actual reign).

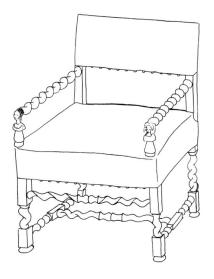

Louis XIII   1610 -1643

Solid, square and massive are the key characteristics here. Twists and turns, carvings and heavy ornamentation with 'grotesque' masks, figurines and cherubs, garlands, bunches of fruit and scrollwork to decorate the dark wood of the structure.

Louis XIV   1643 - 1715

Louis was five when he came to the throne and reigned in person from 1661. Luxurious and elaborate describe his period and Boulle, founder of his own style and first of a line of craftsmen, was his leading designer and cabinet-maker. He launched the fashion for using expensive foreign woods plus tortoiseshell, ivory and brass as inlay; gilt bronze for corner trim, handles and finger-plate decoration; deeply carved garlands, festoons, allegorical motifs and mythological figures to celebrate the power and wealth of the régime, elaborate curves to counteract the solid squareness of earlier times.

Régence   1715 - 1723*

Reaction to the excesses of Louis' court lifestyle set in before he died. The need was for quieter, more informal surroundings. Furniture became lighter, less elaborately adorned, more gently shaped. Heavy, deepset carvings and bronze bits were replaced by flat curves and flowing ribbons. Life, manners and art became less declamatory, less pompous, more delicate.

*Almost a century before the English Regency period.

Louis XV   1715 - 1771

Another child king, he reigned in person after 1723. The Régence search for more delicacy led, under Louis XV, into the Rococo style and the craze for all things oriental - Chinoiserie was *IN* with its lacquer, ivory and mother-of-pearl inlays and lively, exotic scenes of faraway places. Comfort was important too, with fine fabrics and well-padded chairs. So was beautiful handiwork: the period produced some superb craftsmen.

Louis XVI   1774 - 1793

Instantly recognisable by its tapering fluted legs and straight lines, this is the style associated with Marie-Antoinette and the yearning of sophisticated urbanites for a simpler Golden Age when the countryside was the source of all Good, though few actually made the transition. Furniture was often painted in 'rustic' pastel colours, and marquetry was still widely used for more formal pieces. The simplicity of classical forms was the model, inspired by numerous archæological expeditions.

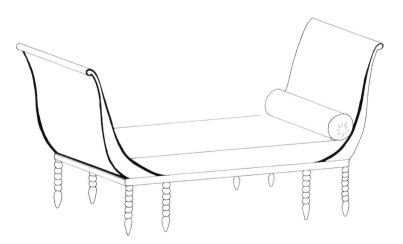

Directoire   1795 - 1799

This is when women started to dress like Greek goddesses and gentlemen wore long flowing coats and high boots. Furniture design continued the trend towards simple flowing lines, less decoration and ever more reference to Ancient Rome (Pompeii revealed its treasures at this time, to everyone's great excitement).

Empire 1704 - 1815

The Emperor was Napoleon I, the inspiration was his booty from the Egyptian campaigns - as well as more Ancient Greece and Rome. Ormulu ornamentation took the form of sphinxes' busts, winged lions and forms were even direct copies from Antiquity. Later, the trend was to over-elaboration and a certain type of decadence.

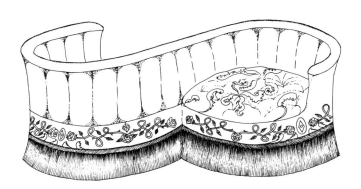

Napoleon III 1852 - 1870

This period, also known as Second Empire, just to confuse you, or the Beaux-Arts style, was the French equivalent of Heavy Victorian. Thick velvet drapes hung everywhere, tassels, swags, fringes adorned them, keeping the light out; the classical style became massive and was decorated with pints of gilding; it used rich dark colours, heavy dark woods, much gilt bronze ornamentation (e.g. little balconies round little occasional tables, elaborate light fittings), veined marble tops on storage pieces.

WHAT TO DO IN PARIS WHEN YOU HAVE MUSEUM INDIGESTION

1. CINEMAS

Programming

Cinema programmes last from Wednesday to Tuesday and each week's listings are available the Tuesday before the new programme starts.

Language

On any day of the year there are some 150 different films showing in Paris and most central Paris cinemas systematically show films in their native tongue' *(version originale)* with French subtitles.

We all know that a disproportionate number of films of all sorts were, and still are, made in English so, if you want to see one of the latest productions or catch up on a golden oldie that you have never seen, cash out on a programme and plan a different kind of culture trip.

Where do I find the information? Two publications excel in telling you what is showing when and where: *L'Officiel des Spectacles*, which will cost you the princely sum of 2 Frs (20 p), and *Pariscope* which contains the same information plus film festival programmes and unsavoury advertisements for unnaturally expensive telephone conversations and therefore costs 3 Frs (30 p). Both carry information on theatres, exhibitions, concerts, cinemas, restaurants, nightclubs, etc.

Which cinema do I choose?

There are a few cinemas that can always be relied on to have good films in their original undubbed versions (look for *Version Originale - vo*, avoid the dubbed *Version française - vf*) The majority of them are in and around the Latin Quarter/St Germain des Prés (5th and 6th *arrondissements*) and we especially recommend the following as places you can rely on to have good undubbed films :

Grand Action	5th	*arrondissement*
Reflet Médicis	5th	"
Action Christine	6th	"
Racine	6th	"
3 Luxembourg	6th	"
Espace St Michel	5th	"
Studio Ursulines	5th	"

IMPORTANT

In some cases, you are still expected to tip the usherette - a modest 2Frs or so will do. If this annoys you, just remember that this may be her only income.

2.   BOOKSHOPS

All other things being equal, books are more expensive in France than in England, not because bookshops are greedier but because books carry a VAT rate of 20.6%.

English-Language Bookshops

Shakespeare & Co., 37 rue Bûcherie, Paris 5th. Metro: Maubert-Mutualité.
A genuine, rambling old secondhand bookshop covering several floors with books stacked on the floor, squeezed into every staircase and more bookcases than walking space on the upper floors. This is a long-standing Franco-American institution where Great Names We Have Nurtured are standard currency and the owner, George Whitman, still holds Sunday afternoon tea parties and poetry readings on the pavement. Mostly staffed by friendly American students.

WH Smith, 248 rue de Rivoli, Paris 1st. Metro: Concorde.
Yes, the great chain has a Paris branch, refreshingly different and independent of the mother house, carrying a large number of books currently in print in Britain and America. Efficient, bilingual, mainly French staff.

Galignani, 224 rue de Rivoli, Paris 1st. Metro: Concorde.
A very smart Franco-American bookshop with old-fashioned panelling and a superior atmosphere. Lots of art books, literature and browsing material as well as normal holiday books. Again, bilingual staff of both nationalities.

Brentano's, 37 avenue de l'Opéra, Paris 2nd. Metro: Opéra.
Big American bookshop: endless corridors and corners with books, magazines, all kinds of upbeat stationery. A must for many - I once saw a Rolls Royce + chauffeur park on the pavement and release two fearfully smart, diminutive women who marched into the emporium of culture with their enormous, gorilla-like bodyguard at their heels.

Tea & Tattered Pages, 24 rue Mayet, Paris 6th. Metro: Duroc.
This is, as its name suggests, a tea-shop which also sells secondhand books. A supremely friendly, student-like atmosphere in a small shop where people come to read (even buy) books and sit chatting for hours

Nouveau Quartier Latin (NQL), boulevard Saint Michel, Paris 6th.
One of the largest importers of foreign books, NQL stocks prescribed
university English course books and a good choice of general fiction,
poetry, drama and travel in English.

French Bookshops

A few are worth mentioning for their wide variety or narrow speciality.

FNAC - the French answer to Smiths, Dillons, Waterstones and
Menzies all rolled into one. There are several branches in Paris (and in
large provincial towns), with big selections on all general subjects and
usually an English-language section -

ÉTOILE	26 avenue des Ternes, Paris 17th.
FORUM DES HALLES	1 rue Pierre Lescot, Paris 1st.
ST LAZARE	109 rue Saint Lazare, Paris 9th.
MONTPARNASSE	136 rue de Rennes, Paris 6th.

Gibert Jeune, 5 place Saint Michel, Paris 5th.
Joseph Gibert, 26 boulevard Saint Michel, Paris 6th.
Both on the Boulevard St Michel, run by estranged members of the
same family, they are a sort of French Foyles who also sell stationery,
records and secondhand textbooks. Much frequented by the student
population.

La Hune, 170 boulevard Saint Germain, Paris 6th.
A lively place just next to the Café de Flore, it stays open late in the
evening and has very good art and literature sections.

La Procure, 3 rue Mézières, Paris 6th.
Specialises in religion but has excellent philosophy and fiction sections
too. Much used by philosophy teachers and students.

La Méridienne, 14 rue du Dragon, Paris 6th.
In a delightful courtyard, it sells books on therapy, spirituality and
modern self-development.

3.   MARKETS

Visit the food markets of Paris to soak up the feel of daily Parisian life -
and buy some of the ingredients that make it what it is. Covered
markets may be in one of those superb iron-and-glass buildings with
masses of stands spilling out onto the neighbouring streets. Some
markets consist of temporary stands set up two or three days a week in
different neighbourhoods. They are always colourful, lively and full of
temptations (plus a few pickpockets) among their amazingly-crafted
mountains of fruit and vegetables. The stall-holders are unlikely to be

locals - more probably from the provinces, suburbs, North Africa or Turkey - and their styles contrast with those of their clients. The last half hour before closing time on Sundays - 1pm usually - can be rich in unrefusable 'finishing up' offers.

Covered markets
Marché Saint Quentin, Paris 10th, Metro: Gare de l'Est.
This fine old 19th-century iron structure, recently renovated, has a wide variety of stalls including Portuguese, Italian, Kosher and organic specialities, hardware and cobbling/keymaking shops as well as excellent cheese, vegetable, fish and *charcuterie* and a café in the middle!

Marché Saint Germain, Paris 6th. Metro: Saint Germain des Prés.
Expensive but very good on fish and fresh vegetables. Also an excellent Greek stall with delicious picnic ingredients.

Street markets open every day (except Mondays)
Place d'Aligre, Paris 11th. Metro: Ledru-Rollin.
Cheapest of 'em all, but make sure of the quality before you buy. Tremendous atmosphere in the crush of eager shoppers, North African voices and spicy smells. The covered market has better stuff - at higher prices. Plus a tempting section dealing in junk, secondhand clothes and crockery on weekday mornings.

Rue Mouffetard, Paris 5th. Metro: Monge.
Super little market at the bottom of the hill on place Saint Médard, and more tempting stands, shops and eating places as you walk up towards the Place de la Contrescarpe and the historic centre of the Latin Quarter.

Rue de Buci, Paris 6th. Metro: Odéon
This is smart Saint Germain des Prés so don't expect great bargains. But a street strewn with banana skins and cabbage leaves will automatically have a relaxed, natural air to it, however Great and Good the individuals lining up for their apple a day. And one or two nice café terraces to sit at in the summer.

Rue Montorgueil, Paris 2nd. Metro: Étienne Marcel.
The last remnants of the old central market, *Les Halles* (aka the Belly of Paris), that was moved out of the city centre in the 70s. The atmosphere is less earthy than in the old days but the pedestrian area is alive and busy and fun to stroll through.

Occasional street markets

Open mornings only (8am-1pm), they are often cheaper and simpler than the daily markets. The best are probably :

Boulevard Port-Royal, Paris 5th. Metro: Gobelins. Tue - Thur - Sat.
Boulevard Auguste Blanqui, Paris 13th. Metro: Corvisart. Tue - Fri - Sat.
Boulevard Edgar Quinet, Paris 14th. Metro: Edgar Quinet. Wed - Sat.
Boulevard Richard Lenoir, Paris 11th. Metro: Bastille. Thur - Sun.

And, although most of the others have one organic/health-food stall, there is one wholly organic weekly market that is really worth a visit if you care about natural food, soap, cosmetics, etc. It is the Sunday morning open-air organic market :
Marché Biologique, Boulevard Raspail, Paris 6th. Metro: Rennes. Organic on Sunday mornings only; non-organic Tuesdays and Fridays.

Fabrics

Cleaning ladies and countesses will go all the way to Montmartre to buy the fabrics and accessories they need for their dressmaking or interior decoration projects. The **Marché Saint Pierre**, a series of shops in the little streets at the bottom of the Square Willette which itself sits beneath the Sacré Coeur, is a Parisian institution. Here, especially at the house of Dreyfus (the wealthy Dreyfus family are more likely to be found frequenting their countess clients than their cleaning ladies), they know they will find a wide choice of reasonably-priced materials.

Stamps and phonecards

There has been a stamp collectors' exchange market on the pavement benches on Avenue Matignon, just off the Rond-Point des Champs Élysées, for years. It has kept up with the times and now deals in phonecards as well. All day Thur - Sat - Sun.

4.   GARDENS

The 'Green spaces' (*espaces verts*) of Paris are few and far between, which makes them all the more precious. Most of them are rather formally French with a small piece called *le jardin anglais* where the rule is to let things look more spontaneous and 'wild' - the so-called English look. More and more municipal gardeners are sowing tough grass seed so that, at last, the French may be allowed to walk and sit on the grass in their public gardens; a few still hold dear the old interdiction and employ whistlers to keep order. Paris gardens are ALL full of people at weekends.

MAKING THE MOST OF PARIS

On the edge
The two biggest green areas are outside the boundaries of Paris proper: the <u>Bois de Boulogne</u> on the western front, the <u>Bois de Vincennes</u> to the east. Both have lakes where you can go rowing, both have quite a lot of drivable roads going through them but still manage to grow more trees and grass than the rest of Paris's parks put together. Boulogne, definitely the smarter of the two, has a couple of famous race courses (Longchamp and Auteuil) and an 'amusement park' - the *Jardin d'Acclimatation* - a deliciously old-fashioned hangover from gentler days where contemporary French children still seem happy with swings and slides and the little zoo. Vincennes, which also has a race course, is more of a people's park and has a wonderful old C17 fort.

Inside the walls *(Paris intramuros = the 20 arrondissements)*
Inside Paris, the <u>Luxembourg</u> garden is still my favourite with the solid old Senate building (Palais du Luxembourg) as its backdrop. There is enormous character in its extraordinarily declarative C19 statues, studied French formality and very staid, definitely pre-90s amusements for children. They come in the form of really slow pony rides and model boat sailing on the pond (boats for hire on the spot - NO motors). The old *chaisières* - 'chair ladies' - tyrants who used to come round demanding a few centimes for the chair you had chosen to sit on, have gone; but the population is still an interesting mixture of Left Bank *grand-mères* and Sorbonne students.

But we must give the next slot to the newest garden in Paris, the <u>Parc André Citroën</u>, way down the river beyond the Eiffel Tower. Built on the site of the old car factories, it is a brilliant study in modern landscaping and theming for a public park. It has two very daring greenhouses and several smaller ones, all built with what look like smoothed-down tree trunks, a series of colour gardens, some fascinating waterworks and a balanced mix of open space and secluded corners. They have even 'created' an overgrown, weedy, 'bomb-site' area. Well worth the trip.

Leading back from the Eiffel Tower, the <u>Champ de Mars</u> was laid out at the end of the 18th century as the practice ground for manoeuvres by students at the École Militaire: it has some nice spots with benches (and uniformed females with whistles to shoo you off the grass). The magnificent <u>Buttes Chaumont</u> (*monts chauves* or bald hills), out in the 19th *arrondissement*, has a series of steep hills (windmills used to stand here) and a reproduction of the Sibyl's Temple - all very 19th century.

Here are two less well-known parks for a change. First, on the southern edge of Paris, the <u>Parc Montsouris</u> is hilly and green and looks natural. Secondly, in the smart residential neighbourhood north of the

Champs Élysées, the <u>Parc Monceau</u> (another 'bald hill') still has the
highly aristocratic bearing of its origins (it was built in 1780 as the
private garden, then twice as big, for the Duc de Chartres' country
cottage).

And there are hidden green treasures behind high walls, inside ministry
buildings, in hospital grounds. Not all are open to the public, of course,
but you risk no more than a stiff watchdog's bark if you stick your nose
in where you're not wanted, so do try. The gardens of the <u>Hôpital La
Pitié/Salpêtrière</u> are a wonderful surprise (and the hospital chapel is
almost the size of a small cathedral). The <u>Hôpital Saint Louis</u> has
unexpected peace round the lawns and flowerbeds of its ancient
courtyards. Built at the same time, in the same style and by the same
architect as the brick-and-stone Place des Vosges, it is also an
architectural curiosity (there's a lot of modern hospital in the grounds
now, too, of course). The garden of the <u>Rodin Museum</u> (only
accessible if you buy a museum ticket) makes a visit there even more
rewarding and the <u>Palais Royal</u> enfolds a delightful leafy and airy space
within its stone embrace.

Last, as in every great city, the cemeteries (*cimetières*) are places of
vegetation, stone and eternal rest and some people enjoy the search for
memorials to Great Heroes (or pop singers, or politicians).
<u>Montparnasse</u> on the Left Bank, <u>Père Lachaise</u> on the Right Bank are
the best known but <u>Montmartre</u> also has some interesting tombs.

How to get there

Jardin d'Acclimatation, Bois de Boulogne - Metro: Porte Maillot,
Sablons. *Bois de Vincennes* - Metro: Château de Vincennes. *Jardin du
Luxembourg* - Metro: Odéon; RER: Luxembourg. *Champ de Mars* -
Metro: École Militaire. *Buttes Chaumont* - Metro: Buttes Chaumont.
Parc Montsouris - Metro: Cité Universitaire. *Parc Monceau.* - Metro:
Monceau. *Hôpital La Pitié/Salpêtrière* - Metro: St Marcel. *Hôpital St
Louis* - Metro: Goncourt. *Musée Rodin* - Metro: Varenne. *Palais Royal* -
Metro: Palais Royal. *Cimetière Montparnasse* - Metro: Edgar Quinet.
Cimetière Père Lachaise - Metro: Père Lachaise. *Cimetière de
Montmartre* - Metro: La Fourche.

5.   WALKS

The River Seine obviously serves as the city's largest lung but walking
along the riverside has been made difficult in the last two decades
because the authorities believed they had to offer as much space as
possible to King Car. Ideas are changing and there is talk of returning
some of those fume-filled water-level expressways to the humble
pedestrian and his dog. The plan, agreed by 'officials' in 1997, is to

provide unbroken pathways and footbridges from the *Parc de Bercy* in the east right round to the *Parc André Citroën* in the west - a 12-kilometre dream. The two islands *Cité* and *Saint Louis* are still good wandering areas too, apart from the main north-south drag between Châtelet and Saint Michel. Guided walks, in French or English, are listed every week in the 'What's On' programmes - *L'Officiel des Spectacles* and *Pariscope*. Here are a very few suggestions from us.

5.1   A new permanent open-air sculpture show has been set up in equally new gardens along the river to the west of the Gare d'Austerlitz below the Quai Saint Bernard. At the end, cross over to Ile Saint Louis and walk along by those fabulous C17 apartment buildings, built for the very high-born and wealthy of their day and still very select places of residence for the discerning. You will reach the Pont Saint Louis which will take you across to the Ile de la Cité and the little garden below the east end of Notre Dame - don't miss the memorial to the Jewish deportees at the very eastern point of the garden.

Walk west along the cathedral, always gazing up at those stone miracles above you, across the square past the hospital that is still known by its medieval name of God's Hostel (Hôtel Dieu) and right for a brief spell in all that traffic until you reach the Flower Market which feels like a slice of tropical jungle lost - and found - in northern Europe. And here too is the *Cité* metro station with its original Guimard entrance whence you can go north or south as you wish.

5.2   As well as its world-famous examples of national building styles, built between the 20s and the 50s to house foreign and French students in an ideal of harmony and international understanding, the Cité Universitaire is in fact a vast 40-hectare park, so visitors can combine culture AND fresh(er) air.

5.3   The deliciously immobile, old-fashioned Canal Saint Martin, which forms a vague perpendicular to the Seine from Quai de la Rapée (one stretch is in a tunnel), was condemned to death by concrete in the 1970s, to make a road, of course, but good sense prevailed. The city now has a stretch of tree-lined water where pleasure barges climb up and down the nine locks, Sunday afternoons are no-traffic times and walking northwards can be most enjoyable, ending with the treat of a good cinema and café on the banks of the Bassin de la Villette. Canal trips inside Paris or out into the countryside along the River Marne or the Canal de l'Ourcq are organised by Canauxrama and Paris Canal, both based at Bassin de la Villette.

5.4   A new 'walkway' has been built on the old overhead railway line between Bastille (just SE of) and Daumesnil. Called the

Coulée Verte (the Green Stream), it is effectively a long thin garden that has been equipped with trees and bushes, benches and entrance staircases and runs all the way at 2nd-floor level above the road. A most original addition to the grass-starved Paris scene and when you have had enough of walking in a straight line you can take the stairs down and visit the craftsmen working (and exhibiting and selling their wares) underneath the arches.

6.   <u>HIGH PLACES</u>

Apart from the inevitable Eiffel Tower (the highest spot at 276 metres but it costs a lot to get to the top), you can climb the steps to the top of the towers of Notre Dame (69 m) for an incomparable view over the heart of medieval Paris and a study of the architecture of the cathedral itself. The department store La Samaritaine, at Châtelet, has lifts to its top floor, a café on the roof terrace and charges nothing for this bird's-eye view of the very centre of Paris (46 m). The Tour Montparnasse is the second highest viewing point (209 m) and has "the fastest lifts in Europe" to its 52nd floor (about 50Frs; open for night-time visits).

TRAVELLING IN PARIS

Our maps are not intended to help you get around Paris. Bring or buy one of the *Indispensable*™, *Taride*™, Michelin or other pocket street atlases and get the excellent map of the metro and bus lines free from any metro station.

<u>Don't use your car.</u> It will cost you a fortune in parking (or police pound) fees and take years off your life in frustration before you find that parking spot. Also, Paris is already dangerously polluted and no-one needs to add to that.

<u>Do use the wonderful public transport system</u>, run by the RATP. It is one of the best in the world. Some bus routes are perfect tours of Paris and its monuments.

The No 24 crosses the Seine twice and runs along the left embankment between the bridges. Other good routes are 30, 48, 73, 82 and 90. Left-bank route 88, the first new bus line in 50 years, has just been opened between the Cité Universitaire and the Parc André Citroën and takes you past Montparnasse and the exciting new architecture of the Place de Catalogne, then on through the conventional residential 15th *arrondissement* to the high-rise buildings of the New Left Bank development called *Front de Seine*.

You are never far from one of the 300-odd metro stations and trains run between 5.30am and about 1am. Many of the stations have been radically refurbished in the last few years and are full of interest just for themselves. There is a brand new metro line too, *Ligne 14*, inaugurated on 15 October 1998. It is a showcase for the latest thing in driverless trains - there will be far more staff presence actually on the platforms - and is designed to take some of the load off the other Right-Bank lines between the new *Bibliothèque François Mitterand* and Madeleine.

Tickets
Fares are paid according to the number of zones crossed. Visitors will normally not go outside zones 1 and 2, the city limits.
One ticket is valid for one journey by bus, metro or RER.

Keep your ticket in case of inspection and to get out of RER systems.
Single tickets cost 8Frs*, a book of 10 tickets costs 52Frs.
A one-day ticket for two zones - *Mobilis* - costs 30Frs.
A two-zone pass - *Carte Orange* - for unlimited travel by the holder (passport photo required) within the two zones for one week: 80Frs per person; for one month: 271Frs per person.
Other formulas for one to five days exist to cover more zones *(Paris Visite)* or to include museum entrance *(Carte Musée)*.
* Prices valid at time of going to press.

Batobus
Not an efficient way to travel but great fun, the 'boatbus' uses the great watery road through the middle of Paris to take you, in six stops, from the Eiffel Tower to the Hôtel de Ville

Bicycles
You can hire a bike and launch yourself bravely into the scrum alone or you can take a guided bike tour, in French or English, from *Paris-Vélo*, 2 rue du Fer-à-Moulin, Paris 5th. Tel: 01 43 37 59 22.
Paris à Vélo c'est Sympa, 37 boulevard Bourdon, Paris 4th, Tel: 01 48 87 60 01, have bikes for hire - folding bikes, tandems, baby seats. Their mouthful of a name translates roughly as "Paris by Bike is Great".

Roller skates and Roller blades
If you want a direct experienceof what lively young Paris is doing today, go to *Nomades*, 37 boulevard Bourdon, 4th, Tel: 01 44 54 07 44. The relaxed occupants will offer you a raft of entertainments:
> • Roller skates and blades for hire at 50-60Frs per day, 10Frs for the armour-plating.
> • Lessons in use of same on their indoor roller-floor.
> • Sunday afternoon 'roller-treks' from their front door.
These draw hundreds, even thousands, of enthusiasts and are free (once you have hired your wheels, of course). They are planning more formal cultural tours of pedestrian Paris for visitors.

- On Saturday evenings, role-play sessions upstairs - costumes and effects of all sorts. All-night sessions once a month.
- At other times, space for card games, board games, etc.

I felt the place had a really good atmosphere. (It has council backing.)

Roller Station, 107 boulevard Beaumarchais, 3rd, Tel: 01 42 78 33 00, also hire out roller skates and blades.

Airport buses

Orlybus between Orly Airport and Place Denfert-Rochereau, Paris 14th.
Roissybus between Charles-de-Gaulle Airport and Opéra, Paris 9th.
Air France buses between:
Charles-de-Gaulle Airport and Étoile or Porte Maillot or Montparnasse;
Orly Airport and Invalides or Montparnasse.
Airport Shuttle is a private door-to-door minibus service that charges 120Frs per person or 89Frs per person for two or more travelling together. Some hotels subscribe to the service. Otherwise, their telephone is 01 45 38 55 72.

Petrol round the clock

Antar, 42 rue Beaubourg, 1st. Esso, 338 rue Saint Honoré, 1st. Total, parking George V, 8th. 168 rue du Faubourg Saint Martin, 10th. 7/11 boulevard Garibaldi, 15th.

OTHER USEFUL ITEMS

Finding your way in Paris is made easier if you know that -
1. The city is divided into 20 *arrondissements* laid out in a spiral pattern that starts at Place de la Concorde.
2. Street numbering is based on the Seine, i.e. streets perpendicular to the river are numbered outwards from it, odds on the left, evens on the right; streets parallel to the river are numbered as the river flows, east to west.
3. The Left Bank is the south bank, the Right Bank is the north bank.

Museum visits are made easy with the *Carte Musées et Monuments*, a pass valid in over 60 museums, worth buying if you are planning to make your visit intensely cultural. Available at museums, big metro and RER stations and the Tourist Office. Price: 1 day 80Frs, 3 days 160Frs, 5 days 240Frs.
The *Louvre* is half price after 3pm, free the first Sunday in the month.

Cookery demonstrations by *Cordon Bleu* every weekday morning. They last 2-3 hours, are given or translated into English and end with a tasting. Price 220Frs. Book 48hrs ahead on Tel. 01 53 68 22 50.

Alastair Sawday's
French Bed & Breakfast

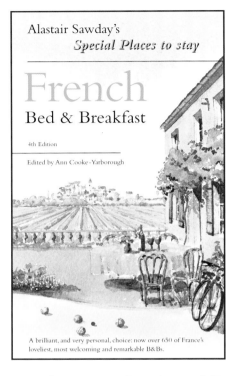

Alastair Sawday's
Special Places to stay

French
Bed & Breakfast

4th Edition

Edited by Ann Cooke-Yarborough

A brilliant, and very personal, choice: now over 650 of France's
loveliest, most welcoming and remarkable B&Bs.

*Put this in your glove compartment; no visitor to France
should be without it!*

It has become a much-loved travelling companion for many
thousands of visitors to France. What a treat it is to travel knowing
that someone else whom you can trust has done the researching,
agonising and diplomatic work for you already. Wherever you are
there will be, not too far away, a warm welcome from a French (or
even English) family keen to draw you into their home and give
you a slice of real French hospitality.

The selection has been honed over 4 editions, and is delectable.
We can **almost** guarantee you a good time! And you will, too,
save a small fortune on hotel prices.

One reader wrote to tell us that we had changed her life! Well, we
don't claim to do that, but it does seem that we have changed the
way thousands of people travel.

Over 660 places. Price: £12.95.

Some of the wonderful places in
French Bed & Breakfast

Spend a night in a French home, be it château, cottage, farm or manor, and discover the French in their relaxed, welcoming reality

Brittany
Les Mouettes

House and owner breathe quiet simplicity. There is light, air and nothing superfluous: carved pine furniture, durries on scrubbed planks, pale yellow or mauve walls to reflect the ocean-borne light, starfish and glowing pebbles to decorate. Pretty village too.

Tel: (0)2 99 58 30 41

Loire Valley
Le Prieuré de Vendanger

A splendid house, with its dormers, balconies and Victorian extravaganza, and a lively, creative couple who fill it with their disorganised elegance: antiques, modernities, Monsieur's murals and sculpture, Madame's relaxation course. They also roast coffee and cook deliciously.

Tel: (0)2 41 67 82 37

South-West France
Le Moulin de Samouillan

The owners left their London jobs in restaurant and theatre to restore this pretty mill in a remote farming region. Their combined skills mean superb food and beautiful decor. Fascinating wildlife, gardens rambling through patio, occasional meditation workshops, too.

Tel: (0)5 61 98 86 92

The Auvergne
Venteuges

Madame is the most natural, courageous sheep farmer's widow we know. If you appreciate genuine simplicity then walk or cross-country ski in this generous countryside and return to a 'cup of friendship', a gaggle of grandchildren, a dated decor and fabulous home-made food.

Tel: (0)4 71 77 80 66

Alastair Sawday's Special Places to Stay in Spain and Portugal

The guide that takes you to the places that your friends would (privately) recommend.

No other guide gives you this wonderful selection of remarkable places to stay in both Spain and Portugal. To the magic that we worked for Spain in our first edition, with its 200 Special Places, we now add the magic of Portugal. Its houses and hotels are quite delightful, with an atmosphere all their own. We have found about 80 of them, great country houses and little beach-side hotels, old religious buildings etc... all of them selected because they, and their owners, are special in some way.
So, you can now find authenticity, character and charm in every corner of Spain and Portugal, and wonderful value for all budgets.
Order your copies from us, or harry your local book-shop. Price £10.95.

Some of the wonderful places in
Special Places to Stay in Spain and Portugal

Discover undiscovered Spain, explore unexplored Portugal - and stay in our hand-picked hilltop castles, cosy cottages, country estates, historic townhouses.

North Spain

La Casona de Villanueva

This grand old 18th-century village house has been lovingly restored and decorated in warm pastel colours, every corner a careful balance of antiques, paintings, fabrics and plants. Attentive hosts, a lovely garden, flowers complete the picture.

Tel: 985412590

Catalonia

Can Fabrica

On top of a hill with heart-stopping views, the friendly young farmers have created a blissful corner of peace and country quiet.
The simple, perfect rooms are smallish, the breakfasts deliciously Catalan, the area full of treasures.

Tel: 972594629

Andalusia

Monte de la Torre

An Edwardian country house on the southern edge of Spain and an English name established here for generations. Here are elegance, heirlooms and period bathrooms, long views, lovely palm-strewn gardens and gracious hosts: a superb place to stay.

Tel: 956660000

Portugal

Convento do Santo António

A Portuguese feast of hand-crafted terracotta and tiles, rich alcobaça fabrics and hand-knotted rugs, this former monastery has cloister and character, antiques and atmosphere, Gregorian chant at breakfast. The 'Special' rooms are, indeed, very special

Tel: (0)81-325632

Special Places to Stay in BRITAIN

Alastair Sawday's

COUNTRY LIVING
In association with
MAGAZINE

Special Places to Stay *in Britain*

3rd Edition

Edited by Jackie King

The guide with 'attitude'... a very personal selection of over 600 of Britain's best private-home B&Bs, hotels and inns.

If you, too, wince at the sight of another lovely old 17th-century room vandalised to make way for a bathroom... then this book (ALL our books) is for you.

Britain is over-run by chain hotels, bad taste and commercial 'establishments'. Even private homes that do B&B are squeezed mercilessly to fit into the mould. So we have searched the country for what WE consider to be the nicest, the most friendly, and genuinely attractive houses, hotels and inns. (Most are very comfortable too.)

Our standards are high: places HAVE to be special. With over 600 special places to stay throughout the British Isles this book is a MUST for the sensitive traveller. This is the 3rd edition of this much-loved guide. Price £12.95.

Some of the wonderful places in
Special Places to Stay in Britain

From castle to cottage, from elegant to simple - a very personal selection of places to stay for your special holiday in Britain.

Somerset
The Manor House
The lintel is carved 1630, the dovecote is 14th-century, the Reformation left a priesthole - this house oozes history. The fine old furniture breathes elegance and peace and the smell of your hostess's baking wafts deliciously to welcome you.

Tel: (0)1225-832027

Devon
Tor Cottage
There is luxury here in fluffy robes, huge bedrooms, a heated outdoor pool and a fountain in the breakfast room. More soothing water runs in the stream and your easy-going hostess can provide inspired vegetarian cooking too.

Tel: (0)1822-860248

Scotland
Chipperkyle
Sensitively restored, Chipperkyle stands proudly Georgian in a superb setting in one of the unexplored corners of Scotland. It is a warm, relaxed family home with children, chickens and donkeys, ideal for walkers and outdoor enthusiasts.

Tel: (0)1556-650223

Wales
Penyclawdd Court
A Tudor manor of staggeringly ancient beauty where every bedroom has dramatic views of the Welsh mountains, the grounds have knot garden and yew maze, the Welsh bedroom is lit by candles. Patina, a sense of history and good company.

Tel: (0)1873-890719

Alastair Sawday's Special Places to Stay in Ireland

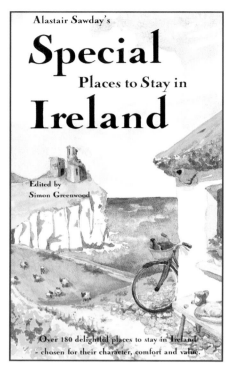

All the magic of Ireland in our choice of lovely places to stay.

Ireland - one of the last havens in Western Europe still unspoilt by mass tourism - is the perfect setting for the fifth Sawday guide. Our inspectors have collected a series of gems that nestle in this wide and wild land where taking in weary travellers is part of the Celtic tradition. The Irish of today are definitely worthy descendents of their ancestors on this score.

Each of the 200-odd B&Bs, farmhouses, mansions and family-run hotels boasts something that makes it truly special - usually a welcome stemming not from the contents of your wallet but from your hosts' genuine enjoyment in meeting people.

We have weeded out any hint of over-commercialism, pretension or half-heartedness in the owners' approach and brought you the loveliest, gentlest, most seductive places to stay in this green and misty country.
Full colour photography, masses of detail, reliable practical information. Available for £10.95.

The Barge Company

INDEPENDENT BARGE BOOKERS

Luxury European Barge Cruises

The Barge Company offers you cruises on luxury 'hotel' and charter barges operating on the canals and rivers of France, England, Scotland, Ireland, Holland and Belgium.

The barges are run by experienced, friendly and English-speaking crews providing high standards of cooking, comfort and service.

For further details contact: The Barge Cruise Company Ltd
12 Orchard Close, Felton, Bristol, UK BS40 9YS
Tel: 01275 474034 Toll free from US: 1-800-688-0245
Fax: 01275 474673 E-mail: barge.co@btinternet.com

Relax, unwind and let the world float by......

Camper
Camp

Camper
Portray (with quick sure strokes)

ORDER FORM for the UK. See over for USA.

All these books are available in the major bookshops but we can send them to you quickly and without effort on your part. Post and packaging is FREE if you order 3 or more books.

	No. of copies	Price each	Total value
French Bed & Breakfast – 4th Edition		£12.95	
Paris Hotels – 2nd Edition		£8.95	
Special Places to Stay in Spain & Portugal		£10.95	
Special Places to Stay in Britain – 3rd Edition		£12.95	
Special Places to Stay in Ireland		£10.95	
Add Post & Packaging: £1 for Paris book, £2 for any other, **FREE** if ordering 3 or more books.			
TOTAL ORDER VALUE *Please make cheques payable to Alastair Sawday Publishing*			

All orders to: Alastair Sawday Publishing, 44 Ambra Vale East, Bristol BS8 4RE Tel: 0117 9299921. (Sorry, no credit card payments).

Name

Address

Postcode

Tel   Fax

If you do not wish to receive mail from other companies, please tick the box ☐   PAR2

ORDER FORM for USA.

These books are available at your local bookstore, or you may order direct. Allow two to three weeks for delivery.

	No. of copies	Price each	Total value
French Bed & Breakfast – 4th Edition		**$19.95**	
Paris Hotels		**$14.95**	
Special Places to Stay in Spain & Portugal		**$19.95**	
Special Places to Stay in Britain		**$19.95**	
Special Places to Stay in Ireland		**$19.95**	
Add Post & Packaging: $4 for Paris book, $4.50 for any other.			
TOTAL ORDER VALUE *Please make cheques payable to Publishers Book & Audio*			

All orders to: Publishers Book & Audio, P.O. Box 070059, 5446 Arthur Kill Road, Staten Island, NY 10307, phone (800) 288-2131. For information on bulk orders, address Special Markets, St. Martin's Press, 175 Fifth Avenue, Suite 500, New York, NY 10010, phone (212) 674-5151, ext. 724, 693, or 628.

Name

Address

Zip code

Tel   Fax

REPORT FORM

Comments on existing entries and new discoveries.

If you have any comments on existing entries, please let us have them.

If you have a favourite hotel in Paris, please let us know.

Please send reports to: Alastair Sawday Publishing, 44 Ambra Vale East, Bristol BS8 4RE, UK.

Report on:

Entry no. _____   New Recommendation ❏ Date _____

Names of hotel _____

Address _____

_____

_____ Tel. No: _____

My reasons are _____

_____

_____

_____

_____

_____

_____

_____

_____

My name and address:

Name _____

Address _____

_____

Tel. No.: (only if you don't mind) _____

Please send the completed form to:
Alastair Sawday Publishing, 44 Ambra Vale East,
Bristol BS8 4RE, UK.

THANK YOU SO MUCH FOR YOUR HELP!

BULLETIN DE RÉSERVATION – SPECIAL PARIS HOTELS
Booking Form

À l'attention de :

To : ....

.... *GRAND HÔTELS* ....

Date: ....

Madame, Monsieur,

Veuillez faire la réservation suivante au nom de :
Please make the following booking for (name):

....

Pour .... nuit(s). Arrivant le: jour .... mois .... année 2000
For   *night(s)*   *Arriving:* *day*   *month*   *year*

Partant le: jour .... mois .... année 2000.
Leaving: *day*   *month*   *year*

Si possible, nous aimerions .... chambres, disposées comme suit:
We would like   *rooms, arranged as follows:*

À grand lit   .....1.....
Double bed
À lits jumeaux   ....
Twin beds
Pour trois   ....
Triple
À un lit simple   ....
Single
Suite   ....

Veuillez nous envoyer la confirmation à l'adresse ci-dessous:
Please send confirmation to the following address:

Nom: ....
Name:
Adresse: ....
Address: *GRAND FRONTAL*

Fax No: ....

Fouiller une question
To research a topic

Fouiller le ceil
To search the sky

Fouiller le sol
To search the ground

Fouiller un suspect
To frisk a suspect

INDEX

INDEX

€ 107

Voltaire?

LA FIN